Communication and Conflict Resolution Skills

Neil H. Katz
Director, Program in Nonviolent
Conflict and Change
Syracuse University

John W. Lawyer
President, Henneberry Hill
Consultants, Inc.
Pompey, NY

KENDALL/HUNT PUBLISHING COMPANY
2460 Kerper Boulevard P.O. Box 539 Dubuque, Iowa 52004-0539

To our parents,
who have encouraged us
in the moral and ethical values that have informed our work

Contents

Preface

This book has been assembled from materials developed to supplement training experiences in communication skills. These experiences were conducted over several years. Initially, the material took the form of charts and worksheets. As particular clients became interested in communications and interpersonal skills training and development, manuals tailored especially to the clients' needs were designed to facilitate the learning process. Over the past seven years, more than 30 different versions of a basic manual were developed, each modified to take advantage of new learnings and insights from the training experiences as well as from research in the field of communications.

Some of the basic concepts on which this book is based emerged from the work of Martin Buber, Carl Rogers, Thomas Gordon, Robert Carkhoff, and Gerard Egan. The communications field has recently been advanced with the work of Richard Bandler and John Grinder, based on their study of the therapeutic techniques of Milton Erickson, Virginia Satir, and Fritz Pearls. The fields of conflict management and negotiations especially have been enlightened in the past few years by Richard Walton, Edward Schein, Joyce and William Wilmot, Alan Filly, Roger Fisher, and William Ury. This book incorporates the best of this research into a readable format that is useful in course and workshop settings, with small groups engaged in discussion or a common task, in counseling, and for individuals interested in enhancing their own communication abilities. Although this book is designed primarily as a companion piece to courses and workshops, it can also be used as a self-instruct workbook, since it includes theory presentation, skill development examples, and self-testing exercises.

Our belief in the value of communication skills training and development has been confirmed by our experience of significant positive changes within individuals and in organizations that have participated in our courses, workshops, work conferences, and learning experiences. These positive changes have sustained and inspired us in our work and provided the impetus for improving our materials and making them available to a wider audience.

Neil H. Katz
John W. Lawyer

Acknowledgments

Many friends and colleagues have helped us in the preparation of this book. It originally began as a series of notes to supplement learning experiences for those who wished to improve their communication abilities. The idea of converting these notes into a communications manual to enhance skill learning experiences originated with Norman Paris and Oron South. We express our appreciation to them for this beginning. Since then, the design of both the supplemental materials and the learning experience itself has been refined over time.

In particular, we thank Fr. J. Gordon Myers, Patricia Livingston, Mary Ulrich, Barbara Roy, Evelyn Whitehead, Jim Whitehead, and Benni Heacock for the wisdom and imagination they each contributed to the design of the learning experience and the materials. We are also grateful to Robert Bolton, Dorothy Bolton, Ed Lisbe, Gerald Hilfiker, and Rick Brandon for insights into teaching interpersonal skills to others; to Dana Hart, Richard Pernell, Felicia Otero, Dudley Weeks, Mary Jane Irwin, John McCullough, Milton Katz, Barbara Duld, and Geraldine Haines for their close cooperation and support in shaping the concepts involved; and to Fr. Daniel Dillabough, Sr. Bonnie Pelloux, Sr. Lea Woll, and Lisa Smith for adapting the material for special audiences.

We are indebted as well to the many people who have participated in the learning experiences themselves and contributed their insights and creativity to help refine our material. We have learned much from these individuals; each in a special way has enriched our lives.

Our thanks go, too, to those who helped us prepare this material for publication: Carol Lawyer, our associate, whose insights contributed substantially to shaping this manuscript; Susan Cohan, our copyeditor, whose patience and commitment to our work have been unexcelled; and Donna Radway, our secretary, whose steadfast services in typing both the evolving communication skills materials and the manuscript itself have been invaluable.

To our families go our heartfelt gratitude for their having stood by us through thick and thin as the manuscript has taken shape. And finally, we especially appreciate Carol Lawyer and Susan Katz for their loving support in this endeavor.

Introduction

The means by which individuals communicate their thoughts and feelings and manage their differences largely determine how successfully they will develop, maintain and enhance their relationships as well as achieve their personal goals. At the heart of communication is speaking and listening. Most people already possess good skills in this area. In normal day-to-day conversation they can usually present their thoughts and feelings clearly and accurately, and receive and understand the thoughts and feelings of others. However, when people are troubled and pressured and are experiencing high emotional energy, they often find it more difficult to communicate. This is especially true in unplanned confrontations. At times like these an individual's own thoughts and feelings might be harder to clarify and present to others, and his or her listening skills might be more difficult to engage and maintain. In these situations people need to be able to call upon a more refined, sophisticated set of communication skills that will enable them to achieve their communication outcomes and help others achieve theirs as well. These more complex communication skills—skills of information sharing, reflective listening, problem solving, assertion, conflict management, and skill selection—are the skills focused on in this book. The effective use of these skills will enable people to turn stressful, difficult situations into experiences of openness and clarity where mutual goals are served and relationships enhanced. This book is used both as a reference in communications and as a workbook to supplement workshops and learning experiences in communication and conflict management skills. Exercises are included in the book to promote understanding and skill development.

Learning experiences which this book accompanies usually involve presentations of theory on communication, practice of skills, and evaluation of progress and results. In such training events, time is provided to help participants focus on their own personal and professional communication interests and specific organizational concerns. A trainer or facilitator is usually available throughout such a learning experience as a resource to help participants address specific needs.

The purpose of the book and any associated learning experience is to enhance your communication abilities and improve your personal and professional effectiveness as leaders. Typically, communication skills learning experiences will provide you with an opportunity to:

- Develop information sharing skills that will enable you to communicate with accuracy and clarity and help others do so as well.

- Understand the obstacles to your individual and organizational communication and learn how to improve both.

- Gain insight into your own communication and conflict-management style and your impact on others.

- Develop listening skills that will give others the knowledge that they are being heard and understood.

- Develop problem-clarification and problem-solving skills helpful in working with individuals and groups.

- Develop effective skills of assertion that will enable you to achieve your needs and interests without damaging your relationship with others or injuring their self-esteem.

- Develop conflict-management skills that will enable you to deal effectively with disputes and differences involving strong emotion.

Coverage and Organization

This book is designed to facilitate learning by presenting practical knowledge and skills in a series of small, understandable units that you can practice, master, and use as building blocks to develop improved interpersonal behaviors. It includes the following components:

- *Information sharing.* You will learn to identify your outcomes in communication and the outcomes of others, establish and maintain rapport, and use language effectively to insure that your communication is accurate and clear. The focus will be on the development of the ability to match another's behavior including voice tone, tempo, and timbre; posture; breathing; and language.

- *Reflective listening.* You will learn about and become more skillful in reflective listening, including the skills of attending and responding to others. The focus will be on developing the ability to clearly hear what another is communicating and understand what is being said at both the content and feeling level. Such skills are useful in helping a person with a problem and are essential for anyone involved in group living and working situations.

- *Problem solving.* You will learn about and become more skillful in utilizing a problem-solving process to help another. The focus will be on the development of the ability to formulate accurate problem statements, clarify problems, and facilitate the problem solving of others. The skills of transferral and referral are also covered.

- *Assertion.* You will learn about and become more skillful in assertion: the communication of thoughts, feelings, and concerns directly, in a way that doesn't damage another's self-esteem or endanger the relationship. You will learn to construct and communicate assertion messages that convey essential information in an unambiguous manner. Such skills are critical when communicating with community or organization members. Since effective assertion is constructive and task-oriented, its use minimizes resentment, passive resistance, and other nonproductive reactions to frustration.

- *Conflict management.* You will learn about and become more skillful in managing conflict. The principal focus is on developing skills of conflict awareness, diagnosis, conflict reduction, and problem solving. You will learn two processes of managing conflicts, one for opposing needs and the other for differences in values. With each process, you will acquire the ability to diffuse the strong emotions involved, and bring about mutual understanding of differences. Then, if appropriate, you will be able to move the conflict to a problem-solving mode so that the parties involved will experience a mutually satisfying solution. In the course of examining these models and practicing relevant skills, your capabilities and personal resources in conflict management will be strengthened and enhanced.

The design of the learning experience which this book accompanies involves building these skill competencies over approximately a thirty-five hour time period, with the skills continually being developed, reinforced, and extended (i.e., well-developed listening skills are required for assertion, and both listening and assertion skills are vital for conflict management).

Learning Environment

The method of teaching skills used in this learning experience involves presentation of major concepts, skill demonstrations, frequent opportunities for guided skill practice by small groups of participants, and general discussions to evaluate progress in mastering skills. Particular emphasis is placed on the ability to utilize skills effectively, especially in stressful situations.

This method calls for you as a participant to become actively involved:

- You will reflect on your own communication experiences and choose a number of personally relevant topics as learning focuses (i.e., areas of concern or perceived need) to guide you throughout the learning experience.

- Real-life communication situations chosen by you and other participants from your personal experience frequently serve as the basis for communication skills practice.

- You will observe skill practice sessions and assist other participants by providing them with constructive feedback regarding their progress in mastering communication skills.

- Throughout the learning experience, you will be given periodic opportunities for group discussion of progress with other participants and are encouraged to share insights/problems regarding the acquisition of new knowledge and the use of skills.

- You will also periodically discuss and evaluate the overall progress of the learning experience with the trainer/facilitator and are encouraged to indicate which topics you regard as being beneficial or not beneficial, or perhaps to suggest changes in emphasis or inclusion of additional relevant topics. This evaluation process enables the trainer/facilitator to modify the learning experience to meet your needs.

Benefits

Communication skills are fundamental interpersonal competencies. When individuals in a family, group, or organization cannot or do not communicate effectively—i.e., don't listen to what others are saying, don't assert in an affective manner, and don't use appropriate conflict-management and problem-solving strategies—the loss is both to them personally and to the larger group. Hence, improved interpersonal communication benefits not only participants but their living and working communities as well.

Some specific personal and group benefits from communication skills learning include:

- Increased overall interpersonal effectiveness.

- Improved ability to reflect and share feelings in a group setting.

- Improved cooperation between group members.

- Improved action planning and decision making in terms of both quality and timeliness.

- Improved ability to listen more attentively and thereby hear more clearly what others are communicating.

- Improved ability to assert in a straightforward manner to get needs met without infringing on the rights of others.

- Enhanced ability to manage conflict more effectively, coupled with an increased resourcefulness in problem solving around needs as well as values.

In the broader sense, when individuals share and communicate effectively, the health of the entire collective body improves, as measured by such factors as:

- *Group/Organizational efficiency,* as measured by the ratio of input to output.

- *Group/Organizational effectiveness,* as measured by the degree to which the group/organization reaches its goals and objectives.

- *Group/Organizational health,* as measured by such factors as morale, creativity, organizational climate and atmosphere.

1
Learning

Learning skills consists of a blend of reflection, sharing, theory presentation, skill demonstration, practice sessions, and evaluation. This structure is designed to facilitate learning in a group setting—a course, a workshop, or a learning experience. Its aim is not to "teach" you, as participants. but rather to provide you a framework and an environment that will facilitate your learning.

A learning experience in communications which this book may accompany reflects certain basic assumptions about the nature of the learning process:

- *Learning is highly unique and individual.* Each learner has developed a personal style of learning and problem solving, which is not subject to imposed modification. However, if the methods of others are presented in a noncoercive atmosphere in which the learner can freely *select* new behaviors that are meaningful, the learner is likely to choose to modify his or her personal style to make it more effective.

- *Learning is sometimes a painful process.* Changing behaviors often generates internal resistance to giving up old, comfortable ways of believing, thinking, and acting.

- *Learning is an outgrowth of the learner's experiences.* Reflection upon the learner's own background of experiences provides the richest and most meaningful resource for learning and problem solving.

- *Learning is a cooperative endeavor.* Learners can learn from and help each other by sharing relevant experiences and by providing constructive feedback to enable others to see themselves more clearly as they really are.

- *Learning requires a supportive climate.* Learning flourishes in an atmosphere of openness and trust in which the feelings of each individual can be freely expressed—an undemanding atmosphere in which alternative behaviors can be tentatively explored, and errors can be made, without pressure to produce immediate results; an atmosphere of tolerance in which differing viewpoints are expected and welcomed.

If a communication skills learning experience is successful, several kinds of learning should result:

- You should develop an enhanced ability to reflect and to share feelings in a group setting.

- You should acquire new perspectives, skills, and understandings. This includes assimilating new knowledge and information as well as developing new behaviors.

- You should develop an awareness of the repertoire of communication skills you possess, including new skills acquired during the learning experience as well as previously existing skills. Awareness, or recognition, gives you conscious control over the use of the skills.

- You should be able to use perspectives and skills beyond the classroom, workshop, or group setting in which they are originally learned. This aspect is often referred to as "generalization," or "transfer," of learning and implies that you can call upon each new perspective or skill and apply it in multiple settings.

- You should develop the capability to evaluate real-life communication situations and select the appropriate skills and behaviors to deal with them.
- You should have confidence in applying the new perspectives, skills, or understandings to specific situations or problems. Confidence is based on your realization that you are actually competent in using the communication skills. Building confidence is especially important in helping participants who become hampered by negative assumptions regarding their inability to perform, when in fact they have merely underestimated their capabilities.

In short, the goal of a communication skill learning experience is to enhance your ability to reflect on and share your repertoire, or inventory, of communication perspectives, skills, understandings, and awarenesses as well as your capability to use these skills with confidence in diverse settings.

Each participant brings to any learning experience unique and highly personal perspectives about self, work, communication—about an infinite variety of interests and topics. Such diversity is welcomed as a significant asset and will be fully utilized as learning progresses. Availability of the rich variety of individual perspectives, coupled with a high level of commitment on the part of participants, will make learning about communications a rewarding and exciting experience.

Skill Learning

The basic method of learning communication skills in a workshop setting is an approach that takes a large category of related skills and breaks them down into simple, teachable behaviors. The advantage of working with small components rather than tackling an entire skill at once is that it lets the trainer/facilitator be much more specific about describing the behaviors and coaching you in their use. Once each specific behavior is learned and mastered, then the behaviors can be combined in many ways to give you a wide range of communication skills.

Generally, each skill component is covered in five steps:

1. *Theory presentation.* You are presented the nature and purpose of the skill.
2. *Skill demonstration.* You are shown the proper way to use the skill with a demonstration by the trainer/facilitator.
3. *Skill practice.* You try out the skill.
4. *Critique.* You discuss your use of the skill, including what seemed easy or hard about it and any new insights you gained from practicing the skill.
5. *Skill practice.* You then practice the skill again.

The difference between a lecture course and a skill learning course is that in the lecture course you are presented with material you have to try to learn by memorization, while in the skill learning course you actually practice new behaviors and learn by experience. Because the opportunity to experiment with new behaviors greatly facilitates learning, the practice sessions are really the heart of the skill mastery process.

Skill Practice

Practicing new behaviors is an important part of leadership and communication skills training, because it gives you a chance to use the skills in a real-life situation and learn about them from experience. It helps to be able to try out the skills for the first time in a "safe" setting, where you are not under any pressure. Instead you can relax and give some thought and attention to how the skills work, receive effective coaching from the trainer/facilitator, and suggestions from other participants on how to use the skills.

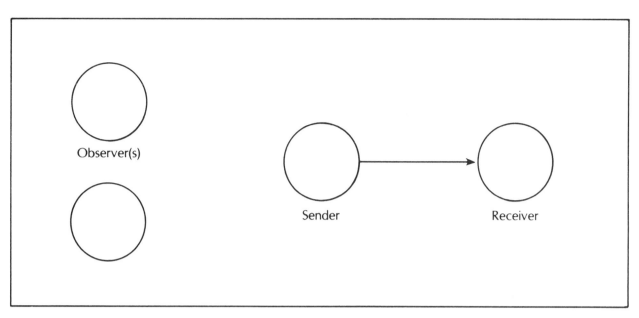

Figure 1. Skill practice.

Table 1. Roles of sender, receiver, and observer in reflective listening and assertion skill practice.

	Listening	*Assertion*
Sender:	Describes real-life issue or problem.	Sends assertion message from real-life situation *using the appropriate skills.*
Receiver:	Listens *using the appropriate skill.*	Responds defensively, without using any skills.
Observer(s):	a. Invites the sender to express how well he or she felt heard.	a. Invites the receiver to express how well he or she felt asserted to.
	b. Invites the receiver to express reactions to the use of skills.	b. Invites the sender to express reactions to the use of skills.
	c. Makes observations and positive suggestions.	c. Makes observations and positive suggestions.

Figure 1 shows how the skill practice sessions for communication skills will take place in small groups of three or four, consisting of a sender, a receiver, and one or two observers.

The roles of the sender and receiver are different for the listening and assertion skill practice. The role distinctions are shown in table 1.

Throughout the skill practice sessions and other learning activities you will be giving one another feedback on your use of the skills, since progress in skill learning is enhanced when feedback and coaching are provided immediately after the skills are practiced. Feedback should be gentle and thorough; and in giving feedback to another, you should try to make your comments specific and descriptive, rather than general and judgmental. It is also important that early in the process of skill learning development, feedback be largely positive: when someone is experimenting with new skills, he or she can easily become discouraged by too much negative feedback.

Skill Learning Stages

In practicing any new skill or behavior, you usually pass through four stages, as shown in figure 2. At first you will encounter some internal resistance to using new skills, because deeply rooted habits must be overcome. This is usually followed by your experiencing some guilt when you begin to consider how many past situations you have handled unskillfully. You then start actively using the skills, but not without feeling quite self-conscious and somewhat phony about the process. Gradually you get to be skilled in the new behaviors, even though you remain conscious of and thus uncomfortable using them. The fifth stage is very difficult to reach. As a result of participation in a communication skills learning experience you can expect to reach the "skillful" stage. In using the skills following such a learning experience you can expect to slip back to the "phony" stage from time to time, especially in stressful situations. It takes a lifetime of practice and commitment to reach an integrated place in anything, especially when it involves changing patterns of communication you have been using for many years. Ultimately, you can reach the point where the skills are so completely integrated into your communication patterns that you are no longer aware of using them.

In the early phases of skill learning, you become aware that your present behavior actually involves the use of skills that you have learned. Once you realize this, you will also realize that it means your present behavior is not just something that you inherited and are stuck with but is instead something you can consciously control and change. This insight will help you "unfreeze" your present behavior and become ready to consider alternatives. You can then examine the need for change; set goals for achieving desired improvements in knowledge, skills, attitudes, and behaviors; and begin practicing the new behaviors you would like to master.

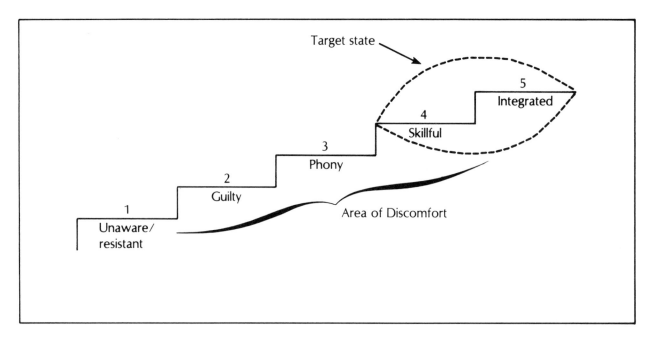

Figure 2. Skill learning stages.

Personal Documentation

You have already practiced techniques of reflective listening, assertion, conflict management, and problem-solving in many real-life situations, and have met with varying degrees of success in using these skills. For instance, you may realize that you frequently listen ineffectively and fail to grasp instructions, while another person may have difficulty asserting to others in stressful situations, or be unable to manage conflict well. Therefore, each participant will have a very personal set of priorities or goals for communication behaviors he or she would like to improve.

In order to give you an opportunity to identify these personally relevant goals and focus your learning experiences accordingly, a process of personal documentation will be used as a learning aid during the learning experience. The following four steps are involved:

1. You will initially be asked to reflect on past communication experiences and choose several expectations of personal relevance or perceived need which will serve as goals or learning focuses.

2. You will then write the selected learning focuses on the following pages which have been provided.

3. After each learning focus, you should add a brief statement giving an initial assessment of your current knowledge and perspectives about the particular topic.

4. Throughout the learning experience, you will be given periodic opportunities for reflection and sharing, during which you can review the material previously recorded and add any relevant comments or new perspectives and insights gained.

The learning focuses and related comments which you record on the personal documentation pages are for your private use only. You will not be required to disclose this confidential material to others during the learning experience, although you are welcome to share the material if you choose.

Basically, the personal documentation process is a means of ensuring that you can monitor your own learning. Relevant goals or learning focuses are clarified at the outset, and learning experience material is constantly evaluated in light of these goals to maximize the opportunity for gaining truly meaningful insights, understandings, and awarenesses.

PERSONAL DOCUMENTATION

PERSONAL DOCUMENTATION

PERSONAL DOCUMENTATION

Trust

Trust is the instinctive, unquestioning belief in and reliance upon yourself, another, or a group. Neither opportunistic nor strategized, it is freely given. When you trust yourself, you are able to fully enter into the process of discovering who you are and can be. When you trust another, he or she can more fully enter into this process of learning, living, and being.

When you enter a learning experience, trust is often low, resulting in defending behaviors on the part of participants (see figure 3). As you experience one another, trust builds, freeing energy to work and play and fully enter into the learning experience.

The trainer/facilitator's task is to structure the environment and activities so that the group as a whole can move into a high trust place where openness to new learning is maximized, where everyone is in a resourceful state and energy is made available for the learning task. A resource state, as defined by Laborde (1984) is "—your optional emotional and physical condition, in which the resources you have gathered during your life are readily available to you."* When each participant in a learning experience is in a resourceful state, knowledge and skills are acquired most effectively.

Low Trust	High Trust
I don't belong.	I do belong.
I will fail.	I won't fail.
I will get hurt.	I won't get hurt.
Energy goes into defending.	Energy is freed to work and learn and enter into the experience.

Figure 3. Trust.

*Genie Z. Laborde, *Influencing with Integrity* (Palo Alto: Syntony, Inc., Publishing Company, 1984), p. 15.

2

Communication

Communication is anything you do to influence another's experience—that is, what is taking place within the other person at both the conscious and unconscious levels. It involves an exchange of meaning between persons in which information is given and received through voice tone, facial expression, hand gestures, posture, etc., so that the thoughts, opinions, information, or feelings of each person are appropriately exchanged.

Effective communication is essential, not only for getting individual needs met and developing significant interpersonal relationships, but also for assuring the adequate functioning of people in any society.

Beyond the interpersonal transaction involved in communication, it can also transcend time and space. You can read and be touched right now by something written centuries ago by Homer, St. Luke, Shakespeare or Martin Buber. You can talk through a sophisticated satellite system to someone in a distant place.

In order to communicate with another, you choose the manner of expressing, or encoding, your message that you feel is most likely to convey your intention. The other then interprets, or decodes, your message and receives some impact from it. The goal of effective communication is to ensure that the impact of your communication on another really corresponds with your original intention and that the impact of another's message on you corresponds with the other's intention. The process is illustrated in figure 4.

The communication process involves use of specific skills that are under your control and that you can enhance. For instance, when sending messages, you can learn ways of expressing your intention more effectively and checking to be sure how you are coming across; when receiving messages, you can learn ways of listening more effectively to be sure you are really understanding the other.

People use language as a way to represent their experience to another. It is a way of communicating your model, or representation, of the world, as you view it, to another. When you use language to communicate through talking, discussing, writing, lecturing, speaking, or singing, you are presenting to another your experiences from your perspective of the world.

This book is concerned about the process of communication, not the content. It focuses on specific skills for bringing about mutual understanding and respect in a variety of different circumstances. The skill areas covered include:

- *Information sharing*—stating your thoughts and feelings to another with accuracy and clarity and eliciting the thoughts and feelings of another to bring about mutual understanding and the satisfaction of both party's outcomes.

- *Reflective listening*—paying respectful attention to the content and feelings of another, hearing and understanding, and then letting the other know he or she is being heard and understood.

- *Assertion*—expressing your thoughts and feelings to another to achieve your outcomes without infringing on the other, damaging your relationship with the other, or injuring his or her self-esteem.

- *Conflict management*—becoming aware of a conflict, diagnosing its nature, and employing a specific methodology to diffuse the emotional energy involved and enable the disputing parties to understand and resolve their differences.

11

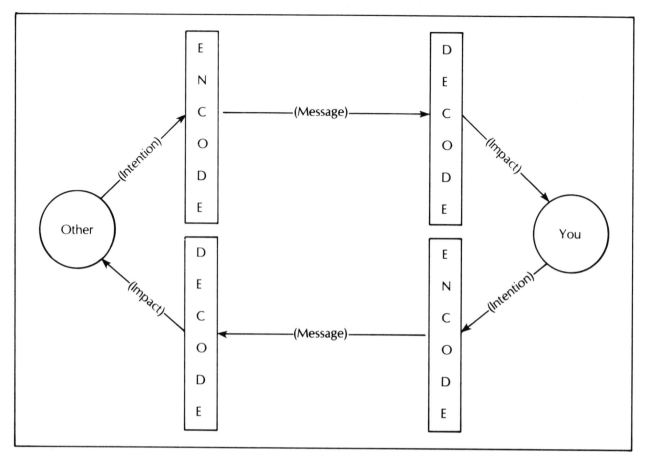

Figure 4. Communication process. (Based on Thomas Gordon, *Parent Effectiveness Training* [New York: Wyden Publishing, 1970], p. 117.)

- *Problem solving*—identifying a discrepancy between a current and desired state and working out the steps required to reach the desired state.
- *Skill selection*—determining which skill area and which specific skills are most useful and appropriate in achieving your outcome.

The first step in becoming an effective communicator is to know what you want—your specific outcome. The second step is to uncover the outcome of the other with whom you are in communication. Successful communication happens when you can achieve your outcome and enable the other to achieve his or her outcome at the same time. This process is one of fitting together outcomes so that both parties in communication experience understanding.

All communication involves either speaking or listening. It involves all the behaviors of the parties involved including the patterns of behavior: shifts, rhythms, repetitions and variations. Speaking is expressing your thoughts and feelings with clarity and accuracy through words and behavior so that the other understands your meaning. Listening is following the thoughts and feelings of another through words and behavior and understanding the meaning of what the other is communicating from their particular perspective or model of the world. The ability to speak and listen effectively to achieve your communication outcomes requires sensory acuity, flexibility, congruence and personal integrity.

- *Sensory acuity*—being curious about and noticing changes and responses in another during the communication process through your five senses—seeing, hearing, touching/feeling, smelling and tasting.
- *Flexibility*—being responsive to changes noticed in another's words and behavior and choosing words and behavior from your repertoire of alternatives to best achieve your outcome.

- *Congruence*—being fully in agreement with all your internal strategies and behavior (i.e., having your internal and external selves in harmony and agreement expressed in terms of words and behaviors).
- *Integrity*—being whole and complete in terms of your spiritual, emotional, physical, intellectual and relational selves and having your words and behaviors in sync with your values.

Outcomes

An outcome is a particular result you want, specified in terms of what you would see, hear and feel if the outcome were achieved. In the context of communication, an outcome is what you want to get from the communication with another. It is like a goal or objective but more precisely specified. In every communication, whether simply exchanging information or managing a conflict, knowing your outcome is essential to insuring that you get where you want to go.

Precisely specifying and stating your outcome, as well as assisting the other in stating his or her outcome, is essential to insure accurate understanding and clarity of meaning in communication. Eliciting and understanding another's outcomes involves:

1. Asking questions that determine his or her desired state ("What do you want?" or "I'm wondering what you are wanting right now.").
2. Obtaining evidence by which the other will know that the desired state has been achieved ("How will you know that you have reached your desired state?").
3. Seeking information that clarifies the context of situations in which the outcome is expected.
4. Obtaining information that indicates whether the desired state is appropriate (ecologically/environmentally).

The following criteria are essential for well-informed outcomes:

1. A specific result
2. Stated in positive terms
3. Specific and measurable in terms of a sensory based description—see, hear and feel data
4. Initiated and controlled by yourself
5. Achievable (manageable size chunks—"bite size" pieces)
6. Ecologically/environmentally appropriate.

Each of these criteria is elaborated, as follows:

Specific result—an outcome identifies a specific result which answers the question "What do you want?". Every communication in which you engage is intended for some specific result known at either the conscious or unconscious level. Getting clarity about the result you want at the conscious level is the first step in achieving satisfaction with your communication.

The other has an explicit or implicit outcome in the communication as well. Eliciting the others outcome affords you with the opportunity to fit together or dovetail the outcomes so that both parties interests in the communication can be met.

Positive—an outcome that is positive will motivate you and the other to move from a current state toward a desired future state. A negatively worded outcome, like "I don't want to feel uptight" will tend to move you away from the uptight state but not necessarily toward a particularly pleasing and satisfying state.

Sensory based—an outcome that is based on sensory experience and stated in words that describe what you would see, hear and feel to be pleased and satisfied with the anticipated result or desired state that is easier to achieve. To get clarity on your outcome, you can ask yourself:

13

- "What will I see when I attain my outcome?"
- "What will I hear when I attain my outcome?"
- "What will I feel when I attain my outcome?"

If eliciting another outcome, you would ask:

- "What would you see when you attained your outcome?"
- "What would you hear when you attained your outcome?"
- "What would you feel when you attained your outcome?"

For example, if an outcome is "to be productive," the see, hear, feel data might look like:

See	Hear	Feel
Book in print	Congratulations by friends	Excited
People in workshops	Positive evaluative remarks	Pleased
New clients	Unsolicited, positive comments	Satisfied

The word "productive" is an abstract word with many meanings. If you know what it means to you in concrete terms, you can more easily focus on the behaviors required to gain your outcome. Specifying it in hear, see, feel data allows you to be concrete and tangible. Some examples of vague and concrete words are:

VAGUE (Words with many meanings)	CONCRETE (Words with more concrete meanings)
Productivity	Apple
Hope	Honey
Courage	Car
Love	Book
Pride	Hammer

In helping another identify a specific outcome in communication, when he or she uses vague words, it is sometimes useful to ask a question which enables the other to completely represent his or her experience (see Meta-Model in Appendix A).

Control—another condition for a well-formed outcome is that it be one that you can control. If it is an outcome of the other party it should be one he or she can control, not a third party. In communication, a controllable outcome might be expressing the benefits of a particular course of action. An outcome that might not be controllable might be convincing another of your particular point of view.

Achievable—an outcome must be achievable or pursuing it will lead to inevitable frustration and discouragement. An achievable outcome in communication is one that is a small enough "chunk" or "bite size piece" that you can accomplish it in a particular communication event. Seeking an outcome that is either too vague or too large a "chunk" is a strategy for disappointment.

Ecological—an outcome is ecological when the implications of its accomplishment are known, that is the outcome is environmentally sound and appropriate at the current time and in the future. To uncover whether or not an outcome is ecological, both the positive and negative consequences of achieving it must be known by you and the environment, i.e., family, friends, professional colleagues, etc. In eliciting the outcome of another, clarifying the advantages and disadvantages of its achievement help the other test the appropriateness of the outcome in a particular situation.

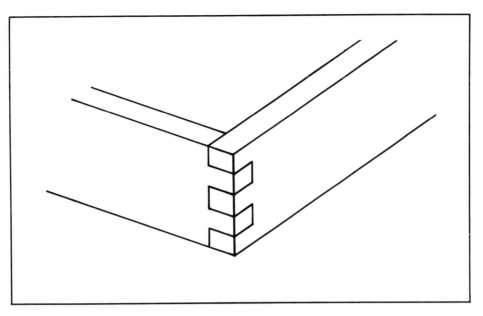

Figure 5. Dovetail joint.

In communication with another, often the only way to achieve your outcome is to see that the other achieves his or her outcome as well. This process is often referred to as "dovetailing" outcomes or "fitting them together." This concept emerges from cabinet making and refers to a particular way of joining two boards together—a dovetail joint, as shown in figure 5. Dovetailing outcomes insures your integrity in the conversation and demonstrates respect for the other person's integrity. Other's will generally help you meet your outcomes if they can see how theirs will be met as well.

Sensory Acuity

Sensory acuity is noticing changes and responses in another during the communication process. The skill involves developing an intuitive awareness at an unconsciousness level of changes in another as communication takes place. As you experience another you form perceptions. Your perceptions coupled with your thinking and language permit you to speak. Perceptions are formed by the information gathered through your five senses—seeing, hearing, touching, smelling and tasting. Language (words) is a representation of sensory experiences. Each sense can be thought of as a window into your conscious and unconscious mind. Richard Bandler and John Grinder have named these windows or modalities "representational systems" and have abbreviated them as follows:

V—Visual
A—Auditory
K—Kinesthetic (touch and feeling)
O—Olfactory
G—Gustatory

These representational systems are the way you perceive and code your experience. Sharpening your perception in all representational systems will enable you to detect minute changes in anothers voice and physiology. Since internal experience (internal thoughts and feelings) is externally expressed in facial expression, breathing patterns and body posture as well as words, you can be aware of minute changes in the feelings of another. The ability to notice changes enables you to recognize when another is, or is not, responding to you. This ability is immensely valuable in aiding you to modify your behavior to elicit the response you want from another in communication.

The most frequently used representational systems for observing changes are visual and auditory. The primary unconscious responses to observe visually are changes in skin color, muscle tension, lower lip size, breathing rate and place in chest, and posture shifts. The primary responses to hear auditorily are voice tone, tempo (rate), and timbre.

Skin color—skin color changes result from changes in pore size on the skin. The blush in the cheek is the most obvious change to observe. More subtle shifts include differing color tones in various parts of the face.

Muscle tension—muscle tension changes most noticeable are those which occur primarily around the eyes, on the forehead between the eyes, and around the mouth. These changes reflect the degree of tension or relaxedness of the other.

Breathing—Breathing can change in rate as well as in the place the breathing is occurring in the body. A person who is utilizing a visual representational system will normally breathe high in the chest; auditory, middle of chest; and kinesthetic, low in the chest or in the abdomen. Changes can also take place in rhythm of breathing.

Voice—voice quality is expressed in tone, volume, tempo (rate) and timbre (degree of gruffness). Changes in any of these qualities reflect changes in another's internal state.

Flexibility

Flexibility is the ability to adjust your behavioral response to another in relationship to changes you detect at both the conscious and unconscious level. If your particular words and behavior communication are not eliciting the response you want in order to achieve your outcome, you need to be able to alter your words, thinking, perception, and behavior until you elicit the response you want. The ability to make the changes and have a variety of choices in the changes available to you is your flexibility in communication.

You can increase your flexibility by deliberately altering your typical way of responding in a situation. For example, you can switch representational systems when speaking, focus on the process of communication rather than the content, or stop what you are doing and try something else in a conversation.

Congruence

Congruence is a state in which all of your various parts, (internal strategies and behavior) are in agreement and functioning together in an integrated way. You are functioning with congruence if what you say matches your behavior and your internal state (feelings). The most important step toward congruence is to know the outcome you want.

The opposite of congruence is polarity. Some examples of possible polarities within a person might be:

Part	*Polarity Part*
Revenge	Forgiving
Formal	Casual
Rigid	Flexible
Independent	Dependent
Learner	Know it all

A classic incongruent response is a person who says "yes" while shaking his or her head "no" or who says "I'm angry" in a calm and mildly relaxed manner.

To ensure congruence, know precisely your outcome and be aware of when you exhibit polarity.

Integrity

Integrity is wholeness or completeness. It is essential for effective communication and achieving intimacy. The key to communicating with integrity is achieving your outcome while at the same time helping the other achieve his or her outcome. The "fitting together" or dovetailing outcomes in communication is critical to each skill area—information sharing, reflective listening, problem solving, assertion, and conflict management.

Skill Area Selection

Choosing the appropriate skill area in communication is related to the emotional energy level—that is, the emotional intensity or strength of feeling—of the persons involved. Making the appropriate choice is a function of your self-awareness, sensory acuity and flexibility. The five skill areas presented in this book are depicted in figure 6 in relationship to the emotional energy of the parties involved.

The first skill area, A, depicts a situation in which neither person feels high energy, and normal communication takes place. This is the area of play, social conversation, and work. It involves the sharing of information and is useful in normal communication situations. In this area, where the feeling or energy level of both persons is normal, it is usually possible to hear and speak accurately and clearly. Each person involved in such situations is usually able to adequately represent his or her experience.

The second skill area, B, depicts a situation in which the other person has a problem, a pressing need, or is feeling high energy on an issue. It involves the use of reflective listening skills to enable you to really hear another's thoughts and feelings and let the other know he or she has been heard. In this situation, the other has a pressing need and strong emotional energy or feelings and requires the support of a listening presence. The situation could be either positive or negative.

The third skill area, C, depicts a situation in which you have a problem, a pressing need, or are feeling high energy on an issue. It involves the use of assertion skills to help you meet your outcomes in a constructive way. In this situation, you have a pressing need resulting from your having been either infringed or positively affected by the words and behavior of another, and you choose to initiate a conversation to deal with that pressing need.

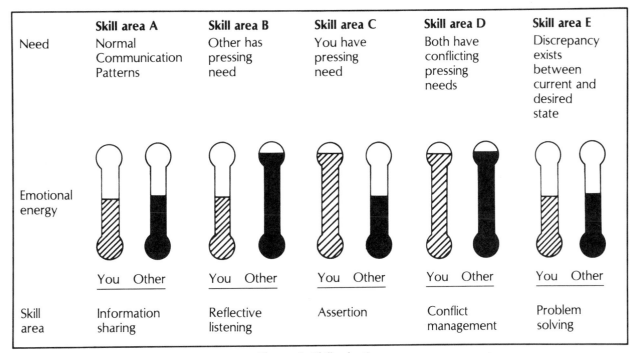

Figure 6. Skill selection.

The fourth skill area, D, depicts a situation in which both you and the other person have conflicting pressing needs or values. It involves the use of conflict management skills to settle a dispute or a difference you have with another in a collaborative way to achieve a win/win outcome.

The fifth skill area, E, depicts a situation in which the emotional energy is near normal but the outcomes desired on the part of one or both parties are still not achieved. It involves the use of problem-solving skills to appropriately help and support another who has a problem or difficulty or resolve a dispute or difference between you and another arising as a result of an assertion or particular stance you have taken that is opposed by the other. In the first instance the other is experiencing a problem that can be solved but requires assistance in finding his or her own best solution. In the second instance, problem solving skills are used to enable both parties to resolve a difference with both outcomes achieved—a win/win solution.

The dominant communication skill involves knowing when to use which of the skill areas in a particular situation. The key is to identify who has the highest emotional energy in the particular situation and determine who has the problem or pressing need and then engage the correct skills to achieve the outcomes of the parties involved.

3
Information Sharing

Information sharing is stating your thoughts and feelings to another with clarity and accuracy and eliciting the thoughts and feelings of another to bring about mutual understanding and the satisfaction of both party's outcomes. It involves representing your experience as well as helping another represent his or her experience without deletion, generalization, or distortion—a skill useful in all communication situations.

Information sharing involves speaking, listening, rapport building and gathering information from another to insure that his or her language is connected to the internal experience represented by the language.

Speaking

Speaking is expressing your thoughts and feelings through words and behavior with accuracy and clarity so that the other understands what you mean. To communicate effectively you need to know how other people process information and how they try to understand. When you know how others process information, you can organize your communication in a way that fits his or her particular way of taking in information, processing it and understanding.

One way of understanding how others process information is to uncover their psychological type. Several models and instruments are available to help categorize a person to understand his or her model of the world better. Popular systems include the Myers Briggs type indicator developed by Isabel Briggs Myers, published by Consulting Psychologists Press, Inc.; the Personal Profile System developed by John G. Geier, published by Performax Systems International, Inc.; and the Social Styles Inventory developed by David W. Merrill, published by Tracon Corporation, Inc. Each of these instruments classify the basic personality type or behavioral style of an individual. Once you know this information you can communicate in a way that best suits that specific personality type or behavioral profile and enhance understanding.

Another and more sophisticated way of understanding how others process information is to observe the specific representational system or perceptual mode used by the other in communication or the specific sequence or strategy the other uses in communication, i.e., visual, auditory, kinesthetic. This method is more precise than categorizing a person by psychological type or behavioral profile because you as a speaker can adjust your communication to suit the other's processing from moment to moment.

Listening

Listening is following the thoughts and feelings of another and understanding what the other is saying and meaning from his or her frame of reference or point of view. When another is communicating to you, he or she is attempting to accurately represent or describe what is being experienced. The experience can be thoughts and feelings taking place in the present moment or a past or future event that is being represented in the present moment. In listening you are attempting to hear the other person's representation of his or her experience with accuracy and clarity to understand the meaning intended.

Typical barriers to effective listening are that the listener talks too much; the listener doesn't listen for long enough before starting to talk; or that the listener remains silent and entirely unresponsive. All these tendencies make it difficult for the other to describe his or her experience. If you as a listener find that you are talking more than the speaker, you may not be listening effectively. The other extreme is passive listening, in which you are too unresponsive to be helpful.

Representational Systems

Representational systems are the perceptual systems through which you operate on your environment. These are the basic elements or building blocks of behavior. These systems include: vision (sight), audition (hearing), kinesthesis (body sensations), and olfaction/gustation (smell/taste). All on-going experiences can usefully be represented in terms of some combination of these sensory classes. Figure 7 describes the codes normally used for the sensory systems and a brief description of their meaning. These notations are used to describe the sensory systems people use to perceive, learn, and behave. Bandler and Grinder abbreviate the expression of on-going sensory experience using the codes ($V^{e,i}$, $A^{e,i}$, $K^{e,i}$, $O^{e,i}$).

SENSORY SYSTEM	CODE	DESCRIPTION
Visual (sight)	V^i	Indicates visual internal sources — images you construct or remember.
	V^e	Indicates visual external sources — images you see externally.
	V^c	Indicates visual images you construct internally.
	V^r	Indicates visual images you remember.
	V^s	Indicates visual images remembered or constructed in space — external.
Auditory (hearing)	A^i	Indicates auditory internal sources — sounds you construct or remember.
	A^e	Indicates auditory external sources — sounds you hear externally.
	A^p	Indicates sounds either remembered or constructed.
	A^c	Indicates sounds you construct internally.
	A^r	Indicates sounds you remember.
	A^d	Indicates internal dialogue.
Kinesthetic (body sensations)	K^i	Indicates internal feelings that you construct or remember.
	K^e	Indicates external feelings that you experience.
	K^c	Indicates feelings that you construct internally.
	K^r	Indicates feelings that you remember.
Olfactory/Gustatory (smell/taste)	O^i	Indicates smells or tastes that you construct or remember.
	O^e	Indicates smells or tastes that you experience externally.
	O^c	Indicates smells or tastes that you construct internally.
	O^r	Indicates smells or tastes that you remember.

Figure 7. Representational system codes.

The subscripts "e" and "i" indicate whether the representations are from external sources, "e", outside you, such as looking at, listening to, feeling or tasting something; or whether they are internally generated, "i", from within you, such as remembering or imagining some image, sound, feeling, taste or smell. The subscripts "c" and "r" refer to whether the representations are remembered from your personal history, "r", constructed, or "c", not yet experienced, like a purple lion.

Utilizing the other's primary representational system involves determining what that representational system is, and speaking with the other using the type of verbs, adverbs, and adjectives that are characteristic of the other's representational system. This allows you to communicate with the other using the kind of language that he or she will find most comfortable and understandable (either one mode or particular combination or sequence of modes). According to Bandler and Grinder, individuals tend to use all representational systems. However, each person tends to use a particular representational system in a given situation or experience—the sensory mode in which he or she is most sensitive and can make the finest distinctions in that situation. For example, one person describing a beach in a visual mode speak about the contrast in colors and hues, the rocks and trees in the distances along the shore and the white clouds and blue sky. Another describing the same beach in an auditory mode might speak of the sound of the waves, birds, and children laughing nearby. A third, using the kinesthetic mode might speak about the feel of the warm sand on his or her feet and the feelings of peace and serenity. Of the five primary representational systems, visual, auditory, kinesthetic, and olfactory/gustatory, the most common with native speakers of English are visual, auditory, and kinesthetic.

A person who is visual would translate information into an image to represent its meaning and tend to rely on seeing rather than hearing or feeling. A person who is auditory would tend to translate information into a sound to represent its meaning and tend to rely on hearing as opposed to seeing or feeling. A person who is kinesthetic would tend to translate information into a feeling and rely on feeling and touch rather than on seeing or hearing. Ideally you should be adept in all senses and be able to choose to utilize whatever representational system is most appropriate in the moment. By habit, however, some people tend to rely on a favored sensory mode to gather information about the world, organize it, and express themselves. This is especially true in stressful situations.

There are two ways of determining the primary representational system employed by another: the first is to identify the "predicates" the other uses in his or her communication, and the second is to observe the other's characteristic eye movements. Let's consider each of these in turn.

Predicates is a term that Bandler and Grinder use to refer to the verbs, adverbs, and adjectives a person uses in communication. These are important to be aware of so that as a listener you can identify the primary representational system of the person you are communicating with and use the same kind of predicates to increase the degree to which you are heard and understood. To help you recognize the predicates that are characteristic of each of the representational systems, we have listed below some typical examples:

Visual (V): see, observe, picture, bright, clear, focus, watch, spy, perceive, discern, notice, distinguish, peer, survey, size up, glare, contemplate, catch sight of.

Auditory (A): hear, sounds like, says, call, speak, talk, listen, time, harmonize, attend, heed, eavesdrop, contact, reach, sound, keep still, keep quiet, register, listen in, give attention to.

Kinesthetic (K): feel, touch, handle, warm, soft, move, rough, grasp, heavy, sad, rub, numb, blunt, sting, thrill, excite, stir, tender, thin-skinned, grave.

In communicating with another, you can use your knowledge of such predicates to identify the other's primary representational system and then speak in that system so that the other will understand and accept your communication more readily.

The second way in which skillful communicators can identify the favored, or primary, representational system of another is to be aware of the significance of eye movements in communication. In their work, Bandler and Grinder have linked eye movements to sensory modes. Using the information they have developed, an accurate observer of eye movements can easily determine another's representational system or representational system sequence and then use this knowledge to communicate more effectively.

Visual

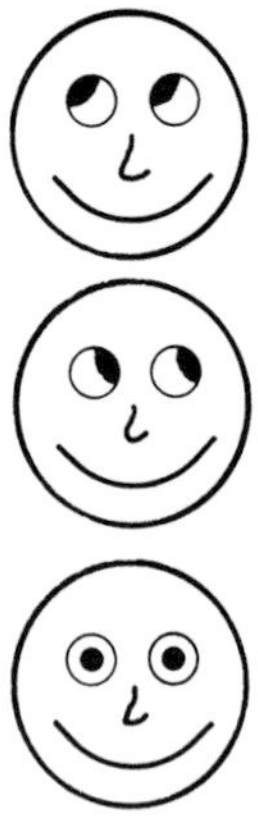

V^c *Visual constructed*—eyes up and to the other's right. The other is visualizing a constructed (imagined, made up) image—something not seen before.

V^r *Visual remembered*—eyes up and to the other's left. The other is visualizing a reconstructed (or remembered) image—something seen before.

V^p *Visual image*—eyes staring into space and not focused, with some pupil dilation. The other is using either the visual remembered or the visual constructed mode.

Auditory

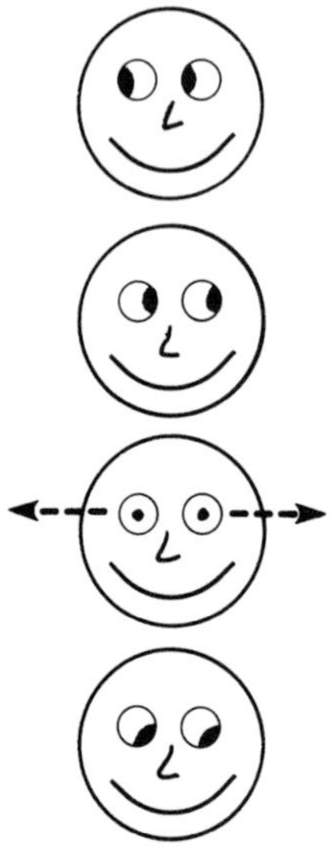

A^c *Auditory constructed*—eyes horizontal, looking toward the other's right ear. The other is making sense in the moment of a sound that has not been heard before.

A^r *Auditory remembered*—eyes horizontal, looking toward the other's left ear. The other is recalling from memory a sound that has been heard before.

A^p *Auditory processing*—eye pupils moving back and forth rapidly. The other is using either the auditory constructed or the auditory remembered mode.

A^d *Auditory digital*—eyes down and to the other's left. The other is engaging in an internal dialogue in the auditory mode—talking to self.

Kinesthetic

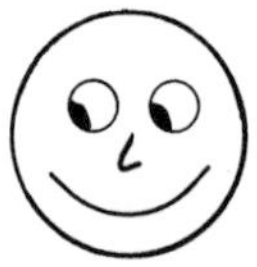

K *Kinesthetic*—eyes down and to the other's right. The other is sensing how the body feels—processing tactile or feeling input.

Figure 8. Eye movement patterns (for right-handed persons).

Typical eye movement patterns for a right-handed person are shown in figure 8. (The patterns for a left-handed person would be the opposite of those shown in the figure.)

By carefully observing the eye movements and hearing the predicates used by another, you can determine whether his or her mode of processing is dominantly visual, auditory, or kinesthetic. Once the particular dominence or sequence is known, you can communicate in the other's primary representational system to express yourself most effectively to meet the other within his or her frame of reference. This allows for more effective information sharing and increased understanding.

For instance, a person says to you, "I saw the best movie yesterday. I focused on the beautiful scenery and the clear, sharp pictures of the characters. I could watch their personalities develop and the plot unfold." In this example, the person is communicating through the use of visual predicates and is also likely to be displaying eye movements characteristic of the visual representational system. The listener who is a skillful communicator could enhance the effectiveness of his or her communication in this case by offering to the other a response such as, "I can see that you viewed an outstanding film yesterday," as opposed to saying, "Sounds like you listened to an important movie yesterday." In the first response, the listener increases rapport by conversing in the same representational system (visual) selected by the speaker—the conversation is in sync. In the second instance, the listener responds to a visual speaker with auditory predicates. The communication is crossed and leads to confusion rather than clarity. Of course, as the listener in the above example, you would continue to speak in the representational system of the other as he or she shares information from his or her experience. In other words, you would match the other's representational system in order both to more clearly listen to the other and to more clearly be heard and understood.*

Rapport

Rapport is a process of establishing a relationship of trust, harmony, affinity or accord with another—a state of special responsiveness. It is a relationship typified by cooperation, agreement and alignment. Rapport is essential for effective communication and applicable to every communication skill area. Rapport is generally established at both the conscious and unconscious level through strategies of matching another's behavior. Having rapport with another results in feelings of comfort, satisfaction and a sense of well being and shared understanding. Rapport is established through reflective listening (see Chapter 4), pacing, and using the other's representational system in communication.

Rapport is necessary in communication to achieve your outcome. If you have rapport, you can proceed with an outcome. If you don't have it, check out the trust level. If trust is not present, find a way to establish credibility, continue with establishing rapport, and then proceed with your outcome. The best way to establish rapport is to be truly interested in helping the other achieve his or her outcome.

Pacing is the key process by which you can establish and maintain rapport. It is a mirror-like matching of the other's behavior and experience as you see and hear it. Using pacing to establish rapport suggests to the other, "I am like you." "We are in sync." "You can trust me." Pacing allows you to make contact with the other's model of the world and to establish conscious and unconscious rapport. Pacing is joining the other's reality in a particular moment. In pacing you can mirror or match:

- Body posture
- Movement
- Voice pattern
- Breathing pattern
- Representational system
- Values/beliefs
- Language
- Emotion
- Content

Pacing tends to minimize differences and harmonize experiences and values. It accentuates similarities and down plays differences so that understanding and rapport is increased and maintained. The specific pacing strategies are elaborated as follows:

Body posture—matching body posture is the easiest but also the most obvious way to pace. To avoid detection, more subtle matching of body posture, such as a tilt of the head or a shift of a hand position, is more effective than a gross body similarity such as matching crossed legs precisely.

Movement—matching movement is an effective pacing technique, especially when the rhythm of the movement is matched with another movement such as matching a head nod with a hand movement. Hand and arm movements can also be matched but only when it's your turn to speak.

Voice patterns—matching voice tone, tempo and timbre is probably the most effective pacing technique primarily because most people are somewhat unaware of their voice patterns. Matching tempo

*Based on Richard Bandler and John Grinder, *Frogs into Princes* (Moab, Utah: Real People Press, 1979), pp. 18–28.

is probably the easiest to use without being noticed. If another is angry and speaks in a loud, fast voice you will need to join the others reality by matching the voice volume and rate to get rapport.

Breathing—matching breathing rate has the greatest leverage in getting rapport because it is the most covert. Once you determine another's breathing rate and rhythm you can pace yourself to it and get rapport quickly.

Representational system—matching another's representational system either in terms of a primary mode used or in terms of the sequence used in conversation is rarely detectable. This means that if the other is primarily using visual, you can match by using visual predicates. Or, if the other is using a V, A, K sequence in communication, you need to match in the same sequence. This can be done effectively whenever you appropriately speak in a conversation.

Language—matching particular words another uses that are highly valued (known as "criteria" words) by the other also help develop rapport. For example you might detect a person using such words as growth, challenge, and integration. These words might be "criteria" words for that person. If you use these same words in conversation, a sense of being like the other is communicated.

Values/Beliefs—matching another's expressly stated values or beliefs also assists in gaining a sense of being like the other.

Emotion—matching another's feeling place can also convey an alignment or agreement with the other. The use of feeling words that describe the other's feelings, whether or not the words are explicitly stated by the other, help convey an in sync sense.

Content—matching the content of another's communication also conveys a common understanding of the experience of another.

The matching of both the content and feelings of another is treated in detail in Chapter 4, Reflective Listening.

Questions

Questions are intended to gather information from another in communication. They can be useful or harmful depending on whether or not they take the focus off the other. If a question helps the other elaborate his or her experience, then it is useful. If a question takes the focus off the other, then it tends to break rapport and divert the other from his or her agenda to yours. Questions can be divided into four categories, as follows:

Open-ended question—an open-ended question allows another to elaborate his or her experience. This kind of question does not invite a "yes" or "no" or a short response but instead encourages the person to fully explore his or her experience. Open-ended questions can assist the other in exploring material he or she might be unconscious of at the time.

Examples of some open-ended questions are:
"Could you tell me some more about it . . . ?"
"Can you help me understand . . . ?"
"I'm wondering about . . . ?"
"How was that for you?"
"What was that like for you?"

Closed-ended question—a closed-ended question limits the other to a short response which tends to divert the other to a different agenda or subject. Closed-ended questions usually begin with *are, do, is, where, did, was,* or *why*. Questions of this type probe for motives or justifications and therefore tend to promote a defensive response in another.

Examples of some closed-ended questions are:
"Why did you take that step?"
"Did you plan to do it that way?"

"Where did you get that information?"

"Are you sure she is the one?"

"Was it your intention to . . . ?"

Challenging question—a challenging question confronts the relevance of the content of the communication to the outcome desired. It is designed to specifically deal with comments or questions which are off the point and have nothing to do with the content of the communication or the outcomes sought by the listener or speaker. The prime purpose of the challenging question (relevance, challenge) is to get the conversation back on the track and directed toward the mutual achievement of outcomes.

Examples of challenging questions are:

"Can you help me understand how . . . is relevant to our discussion?"

"Would you please connect the question you just raised with the outcome we're presently working on?"

"Your last statement throws me—how is that pertinent to what we're talking about?"

"I don't understand the relevance of your last remark to our outcomes, could you explain it to me?"

"I'm wondering if you could connect me with how what you just said fits in our conversation right now?"

Specifying question—a specifying question enables another to more explicitly represent his or her experience with accuracy and clarity. Specifying questions elicit from another a full and complete representation of experience, challenge limitations in the other's model of the world, or challenge semantically ill-formed sentences in the other's communication. They are extremely useful in helping another get in touch with the specifics of a concern or problem.

Examples of specifying questions are:

"About whom?" or "Of whom?"

"About what?" or "Of what?"

"What specifically?"

"How specifically?"

"What would happen if . . . ?"

"All?" "Never?" "Always?"

"Better than what/who specifically?"

These questions which can sometimes come across as blunt, are best asked in a gentle way, such as:

"I'm wondering what, specifically, you mean by . . . ?"

"I'm curious about. . . ."

"Would you be willing to tell me how, specifically, you. . . ."

"I'm wondering if . . . ?"

"Could you help me understand . . . ?"

The specifying question emerged in the work of John Grinder and Richard Bandler as the Meta Model . . . "an explicit set of linguistic information-gathering tools designed to reconnect a person's language to the experience represented by his or her language." The Meta-Model was developed from the insights of A. Korzybski and N. Chomsky, and originally presented in the two volumes of *The Structure of Magic.**

A. Korzybski initially developed the concept that a map of something is not the same thing as the territory it represents. Similarly, language is not experience but a representation of experience and, like a map, is a representation of a territory. As you experience life you will always be experiencing the map or your perception of the territory and not the territory itself. As you change, your experience or perception of the world changes, not the world itself.

Each individual develops a model or map of the world to guide behavior and make sense out of his or her experience. To create a model, your internal experience must interact continually with your external or sensory experience.

*John Grinder and Richard Bandler, *The Structure of Magic* I and II, (Palo Alto: Science and Behavior Books, Inc., 1975), page 35.

Your behavior makes sense only when viewed in the context of the choices generated by your model of the world. The choices you make are always the best available from your particular model of the world. It is, however, possible for your model of the world to be lacking in useful choices as a consequence of malfunctions in your perceptual or thinking processes.

Models of the world are created through three universal human modeling processes; deletion, generalization and distortion. These processes allow you to function effectively in the world. If, however, you mistake your perception of reality for reality, the processes of deletion, generalization and distortion limit your ability to survive, learn, develop, understand, and experience the richness of life.

Language, as a system for representing human experience, is subject to inappropriate deletion, generalization and distortion. Each of these universal modeling processes are examined in this section.

Deletion is the process by which you selectively pay attention to certain aspects of your experience and exclude others. In deletion, something is missing from your representation of your experience; your communication is missing some elements and is therefore incomplete.

Deletion can have both positive and negative results. For example, in listening to another in a restaurant, you can delete all sounds other than the voice of the person you are listening to—a very useful ability. However, if you delete all affirmative, caring remarks of others, your self-esteem might be diminished.

Suppose someone says to you, "I'm scared." The words *I'm scared* leave out the object of the fear and are an incomplete communication. "I'm scared of nuclear holocaust," however, might more fully represent the other's fear.

Generalization is the process by which an element of your experience becomes detached from the original experience and begins to represent an entire category of which the particular element of your experience is an example.

Generalization has both useful and potentially nonuseful results. For example, if you get into an argument with a police officer over whether you were going ten miles per hour or fifteen miles per hour over the speed limit, and he or she becomes upset and charges you with resisting an officer as well as speeding, you can generalize that arguing with police officers is not productive—a useful learning. You can modify your behavior as a result of that experience and avoid arguing with police officers in the future. However, if you were to go so far as to generalize that all attempts to explain your position to a police officer are to be avoided, your generalization might not be useful.

Suppose that someone says to you, "I don't trust people." The word *people* is a generalization and an incomplete representation of the other's experience. In order for the other to completely represent his or her experience, the specific person or persons involved need to be specified in the communication.

Distortion is the process which allows you to make a shift in your experience of sensory data. Distortion also has useful and potentially non-useful results. For example, you cannot envision a desired future without the ability to distort reality. A novel is a misrepresentation of reality in fiction, yet very enjoyable to read. However, if you distort all negative feedback as "I'm unlovable," the constructive value of feedback for growth and change is lost.

Another example of distortion is when you perceive something as being finally determined when it is in fact still in process. Distortion in this instance is an incomplete representation of your experience because you lose control of an ongoing process by portraying it as an event that necessarily occurs with a fixed outcome, where nothing can be done to change it.

Suppose someone says to you, "I really regret my decision." The word *decision* implies that the topic has been settled and is not open for consideration. The decision may in fact be appropriate and the representation of experience accurate. In many cases, however, another may represent an experience as final when it is actually not yet complete. In such cases the communication is incomplete, in that it does not truly represent the person's experience.

Because these three universal modeling processes are expressed in language patterns, you can use the Meta-Model to challenge them when they are found to limit rather than expand another's behavioral choices. In this way you invite the other to reconnect his or her language to the experience that is represented by the language. The Meta-Model distinctions are further elaborated in Appendix A.

4
Reflective Listening

Listening was defined earlier as following the thoughts and feelings of another and understanding what the other is saying from his or her perspective. Reflective listening is a special type of listening that involves paying respectful attention to the content and feelings expressed in another's communication, hearing and understanding, and then letting the other know that he or she is being heard and understood. It requires responding actively to another while keeping the focus of your attention totally on him or her. It includes not only listening to the words and the body language but listening with a kind of total perceptiveness. In reflective listening you do not offer your perspective but carefully keep the focus on the other's need or problem. The process consists of two moments:

1. Really hearing and understanding what the other person is communicating through words and body language.
2. Reflecting (saying to the other) succinctly the thoughts and feelings you heard through your own words, tone of voice, body posture, and gestures, so that the other knows he or she is being heard and understood.

In order for this process to be effective, you must be able to perceive accurately what the other is experiencing and communicating; understand the communication at both the content and feeling level; accept the other's feelings; and, if there is a problem, commit to be present to the other while he or she works through that problem and arrives at a solution. When you can answer the question "What is going on with this person right now?" then you are listening with all your perceptual capacities.

Reflective listening can be grouped into two skill clusters:

- *Attending skills*—the skills of posture, physical contact, gestures, interested silence, acknowledgement responses, and selecting an appropriate environment. These responses are used throughout the reflective listening process, as appropriate.
- *Responding skills*—the skills of reflecting or expressing to the other the essence of the content, feelings, and meanings you hear as well as summarizing larger segments of what is said. These responses are used throughout the exchange whenever a significant segment of the communication is heard.

Important to reflective listening is "chunk size." In this context, a chunk is a small segment of a communication that captures a thought, feeling or meaning, or several thoughts, feelings or meanings that fit together with a theme or are connected in some specific way. In reflective listening you will ordinarily listen to a "chunk" or "bite size piece" of the other's communication and express or state the essence of it to the other in your own words. The "chunking down" of another's communication into such small pieces allows you to digest a workable amount of content and feelings. With such "chunking down", both parties in a communication don't have to focus their cognitive abilities on the whole communication but only manageable segments. The process of "chunking down" the other's communication is illustrated in figure 9.

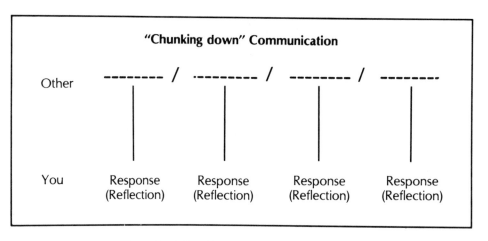

Figure 9. ``Chunking down'' communication.

Reflective listening is useful in a variety of situations, including:

1. Helping when another is experiencing a difficulty or problem.
2. Problem solving, assertion, conflict management, and negotiation.
3. Creating a climate of warmth and welcoming.
4. Reading others' nonverbal signs and energy level.
5. Handling resistance or anger.
6. Settling disputes and differences.
7. Leading group discussions/conversations.
8. Clarifying directions.
9. Offering short acknowledgments in a conversation.
10. Conducting a difficult conversation with another.

The reflective listening process offers a number of benefits:

1. It lets the other person realize he or she has been heard, understood, cared for, and supported.
2. It gives the other feedback on what he or she said and how it came across.
3. It lets you check your own accuracy in hearing what the other has said.
4. It avoids the illusion of understanding.
5. It helps prevent "mental vacation" (discussed in the later section on Responding Skills and illustrated in figure 11).
6. It helps the other focus on self, ventilate, sort out issues, discharge and express feelings, and deal more effectively with emotions.
7. It allows the other to move to deeper levels of expression at his or her own pace.
8. It helps the other to think and articulate more clearly.
9. It helps the other arrive at a solution to his or her own problem.
10. It helps you clarify what you are expected to do.
11. It helps you deal effectively with the problem and needs of the other person or with the issue the other has raised.

Attending Skills

Attending is giving your physical and psychological attention to another person in a communication situation. Effective attending conveys nonverbally that you are interested and are paying careful attention to the other.

Effective physical attending takes place when you adopt a posture of involvement which includes facing the person speaking to you and leaning slightly toward him or her, establishing good eye contact, avoiding distractions, interested silence, and arranging to have an appropriate environment for the conversation.

The following are several components of attending:

- *Contact.* Eye contact is one way of indicating interest in the other person, because the eyes are one of the key modes of communication. This does not mean that eye contact must be a fixed stare to be effective. If you are honestly interested and at ease, you will look naturally at the other throughout the communication. Another element of contact is the distance between yourself and the other person. It is important to base this on the comfort level of the other person. Some experimentation is usually necessary before two people discover the most comfortable distance between themselves.

- *Posture.* Usually, when you are listening, you lean slightly toward the person speaking to you. It is important that your manner be relaxed, because tenseness tends to take the focus off the other. An open posture is a sign that you are mentally receptive to what the other has to say. You should, of course, face the other person during the conversation.

- *Gestures.* You communicate a great deal by your body movements when you are listening to another. If you get fidgety, drum your fingers on the chair, cross your arms, or sneak glances at your watch, you might be conveying an unintended message to the other person. The key to effective use of gestures is to avoid motions that might be distracting.

- *Environment.* The environment, or setting, should be supportive of the communication. A space that promotes privacy for undisturbed conversation is essential. You should remove barriers between yourself and the person you are listening to (such as a large table that comes between you, a car door you might be leaning on, or a crowd that happens to surround you at the moment) or— if that is not possible—choose an alternate space or a more appropriate time.

- *Interested silence.* A period of active, attentive silence serves as a gentle nudge to the other to move deeper into the conversation. It allows the other time to think and reflect and then comfortably proceed at his or her own pace. Giving the other time in which to experience and explore the feelings that churn up from within often enables the other to explore his or her feelings at a deeper level. Silence is particularly useful in situations of loss or grief, such as the death of a loved one or a significant personal loss. Appropriate silence is useful in helping the other talk about a difficult problem.

The underlying message in attending is that both your physical presence and what you say matter. Always adjust the intensity of your attending to the other's level of comfort. In attending, as well as in responding: *Keep the focus on the other.*

Responding Skills

Responding skills are reflections of the content, feelings, or meaning of another's experience. In responding you attempt to express to the other the essence of both the content and the feeling the other has communicated to you. As the listener, your response is short, succinct, and stated in your own words.

Responding skills are broken down into five categories:

- *Acknowledgment responses.* Acknowledgment responses are brief, one- to three-word statements or nonverbal gestures to demonstrate to another that you are following the conversation. Such responses help the other know he or she is being heard. Examples are:

Um-hmmm.	How about that!
Un-huh.	Go on.
I see.	Really.
Oh.	Yeah.
Sure.	You did, eh?
You betcha!	Yes.
No fooling!	Sounds good.
Right.	Right on!

- *Reflecting content*—in which you listen accurately to another person and reflect the essence of the *content* of the communication to the other in your own words.

- *Reflecting feelings*—in which you listen accurately to another person and reflect the *feeling component* of the communication to the other in your own words.

- *Reflecting meanings (combining feelings and content)*—in which you listen accurately to another person and reflect the essence of *both the content and the feelings* that the other has expressed.

- *Summarizing*—in which you listen accurately to another person and reflect the *main points* of the other's communication in a succinct yet comprehensive manner. Summarizing condenses all of what a person has said into two or three sentences.

The responding process requires that the other's communication be heard in manageable "chunks." Following each significant "chunk" you as a responder express your perception of the essence of that chunk to "check" the accuracy of your listening, as shown in figure 10.

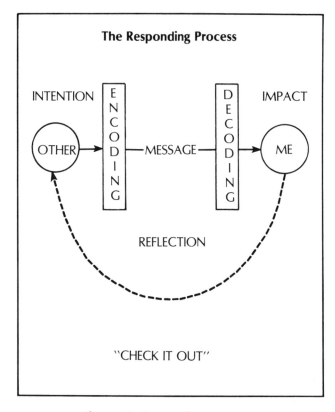

Figure 10. Responding process.

30

Your expression or statement to the other provides a check to insure that you are hearing accurately and clearly and to let the other know that you are understanding what he or she is communicating. Your reflection (statement or expression of this essence of a specific chunk of communication) to the other literally is heard by the other at the unconscious level. If it fits with the speaker's model of the world at that moment, he or she will continue the conversation without a break. If the reflection is somewhat "off target," the speaker will become conscious of the mis-match at the conscious level and make the necessary correction, for example "No, that's not quite right. I think it's more like irritation." If the reflection is completely "off target," it diverts the conversation and takes the focus off the other.

In using the responding skills you will often literally "break in" to the other's communication. This is experienced as interruptive only if your reflection misses the essence of the other's communication. If your reflection is accurate, the intervention is experienced as facilitative.

The responding process involves four steps:

Taking in cues. As another communicates, you listen for and record cues in three areas:
- Content—the content of the communication.
- Feelings—the feelings implied in the communication.
- Context—the external environment surrounding the communication.

Sorting. Sifting through the cues to arrive at a judgment about what is the essence of a particular "chunk" of the communication.

Drawing a conclusion. Determining what the essence of the communication is.

Expressing the essence. Stating the essence of a "chunk" of the communication to the other in your own words to "check out" whether or not you are understanding the other.

Responding skills are appropriate for behavior as well as words; with behavior you reflect what you see. A "door opener" is one example of a situation where there are usually no words to reflect, only behavior.

A "door opener" is a noncoercive invitation extended to another to talk—an invitation to get started. It is a statement that expresses your perception of what the other is thinking or feeling. A door opener is usually a reflection of only the behavior you see because often no words are expressed. Door openers involve four steps:

1. Reflect what you see (behavior).
2. Invite to talk, either stating or implying that you are able and willing to take time to listen.
3. Wait in silence to allow the other to initiate communication.
4. Reflective listen, as appropriate.

Some examples of door-openers are:

- You seem troubled.
- You sure look excited.
- You're really annoyed.
- You appear upset about something.
- It seems like things really went well.

Communication leads are phrases that are sometimes useful in introducing a reflection in the responding process. They can be grouped into two categories:

1. *Where perceptions appear accurate.* These are phrases that are useful when you trust that your perceptions of what the other person is trying to say are accurate, and the other is receptive to your listening:

   "From your point of view . . ."
   "It seems to you . . ."
   "In your experience . . ."

"As you see it . . ."
"You think . . ."
"You believe . . ."
"You figure . . ."

2. *Where perceptions appear clouded.* These are phrases that are useful when you are having some difficulty perceiving clearly what the other person is trying to say, or it seems that the other might not be receptive to your listening:

"It seems like . . ."
"What I guess I'm hearing is that you or you're . . ."
"It appears that you . . ."
"It might be that you . . ."

Responding skills can generally be applied appropriately in the following situations:

1. When the person you are listening to has a strong need to be heard, and you feel accepting of him or her. (The intensity of the speaker's emotions indicates whether or not there is a strong need.)

2. When you are confused about what another person is trying to say to you.

3. When you are listening to another person, and you agree to do something. In such cases, it is often very helpful for you to reflect back to the other what it is you think you agreed to, just to confirm your understanding of what will be involved. Even though two or more parties may *think* they are mutually agreed on doing something, unless an effective listener among them takes the opportunity to reflect the specifics of the agreement back to the other(s), it frequently ends up with the parties involved walking away from the exchange with conflicting understandings and differing interpretations.

In practicing responding skills real problem situations are used to enable the person practicing the skills to experience the energy and feeling of the other. The best situations for practice in a learning experience that this book accompanies are medium emotional level situations. Appropriate situations include an unresolved problem or a recent positive experience.

Reflecting Content

Reflecting content is listening accurately to another person and reflecting the essence of the content of the communication to the other in your own words. In reflecting content, you focus on the content of what a speaker is saying to you, including thoughts, ideas, beliefs, facts, data, etc. In content reflection the focus is the thoughts and ideas of the other—the subject of a particular chunk of a communication. The process involved in reflecting content is using the responding process with an emphasis on the content of the communication.

Reflecting content can be useful in:

• Enabling you to check your understanding of the content of what is being communicated to you. This includes clarifying understandings, plans, and agreements in both interpersonal and group settings.

• Enabling the other to know that he or she has been heard and understood.

• Providing an atmosphere of freedom that allows the other person to explore concerns, issues, and problems in his or her life.

• Letting the other person know you are listening and are interested in him or her and in what is being expressed, thereby communicating respect to the other.

• Reducing repetition on the part of the other person, because you are able to confirm to him or her your understanding of what was said to you.

• Letting you give the other feedback on how he or she is coming across, which often allows the other to gain new insights as a result of the reflective listening process.

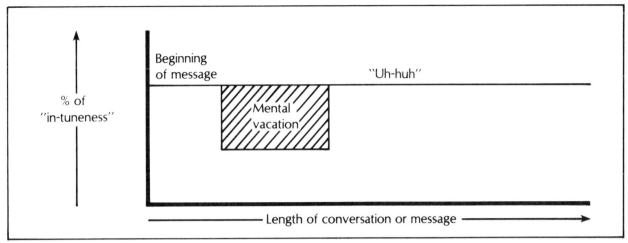

Figure 11. Mental vacation.

- Helping the other person gain direction and work toward a solution to a concern or problem being experienced.

Significant applications for reflecting content include:

- Fielding questions raised in a group setting so that you may be certain you are answering the correct question.
- Clarifying directions so that you can proceed to take the appropriate action.
- Grasping quickly the essence of the content of the conversation before moving into an intense listening situation.
- Conducting content-centered discussions to ensure understanding of various points made.
- Facilitating a problem-solving process with another.
- Handling resistance, anger and hostility, and other negative feelings.
- Managing conflicts to clarify the other's position, interests and values in the dispute.

Often when someone is either communicating rapidly to you or conveying a lot of information, you can develop the tendency to "tune out" of the conversation and check back in occasionally with an "uh-huh." The skill of reflecting content helps you avoid taking this sort of "mental vacation" when listening to another.

Figure 11 illustrates this "tune-out" period. The vertical axis represents the percentage of "in-tuneness," and the horizontal axis represents the length of the message. When shown on a graph like this, it becomes easy to see how your attention tends to decrease as the duration of the conversation increases. Reflecting content, then, is a simple way for you to avoid "tuning out" partway through a conversation.

Please complete the Reflecting Content Responses column in the *Responding Skills Worksheet* section in this chapter. Read each statement carefully and, in the space provided, write your reflecting content response. Typical responses are included following the worksheet.

Reflecting Feelings

Reflecting feelings is listening accurately to another and reflecting the feeling component of the communication to the other in your own words. It involves stating succinctly a feeling word that captures the emotion of the other. This verbal reflection is often accompanied by a mirroring in facial expression, voice tone, and body language of the other. It involves expressing in your own words the essential feelings stated or strongly implied by the other.

The purpose of reflecting feelings is to bring vaguely expressed feelings into clearer awareness. So often, others talk about their feelings as "it" or "them," as if feelings were not part of themselves. Reflecting feelings assists the other to "own" his or her feelings. Feelings are generally more central than content in another's communication.

There is great value in hearing both negative and positive feelings:

Negative Feelings

When negative feelings are heard, they lessen and heal, and there is room for others.

Positive Feelings

When positive feelings are heard, they deepen and become integrated.

In using feeling reflections, begin your response as follows:

"You feel . . ."   "You sound . . ."   "You look . . ."

"You're feeling . . ."   "You're sounding . . ."   "You're looking . . ."

This helps the other to get in touch with and own the feeling and represent his or her experience accurately. In reflecting feelings, it is important to keep a tentative flavor and always allow time for the other to correct your reflection if it is inaccurate.

The skillful use of reflecting feelings depends on the listener's ability to identify feelings and cues for feelings. Some feelings are more subtle than others. Feelings of love, hate, disgust, fear, or anger are examples of strong feelings that usually do not need reflecting, in that the other is usually well in touch with them. More subtle feelings—such as affection, pleasure, hostility, guilt, or anxiety—are often disguised behind nonfeeling words. As a listener, look for the hidden feelings and bring them out in the open for the other to recognize more clearly, using the following formula:

1. Look at the other's physical signs (energy, body, facial expression).

2. Pay attention to verbal signs (tone, rate, volume, inflection, feeling words, content).

3. Ask yourself, "How would I feel?"

4. Say "You feel _____" or "You're feeling _____."

In feeling reflection the focus is the emotion of the other. The process involved in reflecting feelings is using the responding process with emphasis on the kinesthetic component of the conversation.

Emotion is energy level. Feelings are the values we assign to the energy level, and feeling words are our means of expressing these values. But because our feeling vocabularies are limited, we often describe feelings imprecisely, settling for a mild adjective like *upset,* for instance, when we really mean *furious.* A list of feeling words is included in Appendix B to help you increase your feeling vocabulary.

Please complete the Reflecting Feelings Responses column in the *Responding Skills Worksheet* section in this chapter. Read each statement carefully and, in the space provided, write your response, focusing on the feeling component of the other's statement. Typical responses are included following the worksheet.

Reflecting Meanings

Reflecting meanings is listening accurately to another and reflecting both the content and feeling of the other in a single response. The content and feeling can be tied together using such words as *because* or *when.* The skill involves understanding and reflecting both the feeling and the related content of the other's communication in the listener's own words. The following formulas can be used:

"You feel __(feeling word)__ because ____(content)____."

"You feel _____ about _____."

"You feel _____ when _____."

"You feel _____ that _____."

Please complete the Reflecting Meanings Responses column in the *Responding Skills Worksheet* section in this chapter. Read each statement carefully and, in the space provided, write your response, combining a content and feeling reflection. Typical responses are included following the worksheet.

Responding Skills Worksheets

Directions

This worksheet is designed for practicing the writing of reflective listening responses. The first pages provide spaces for your responses to fifteen situations, including:

Column 2—Reflecting Content Responses

Column 3—Reflecting Feelings Responses

Column 4—Reflecting Meanings Responses

The spaces for your responses are followed by a listing of example responses to each of the situations.

WORKSHEET

Situation	Reflecting content response	Reflecting feelings response	Reflecting meanings response
1. These meetings continually last an hour or more over the allotted time, and I can't take that kind of time.			
2. I wish I were more accepted by the professor. I have a lot to contribute but just don't get called on much.			
3. I prepared and prepared for the exam next week. I just think I'm going to fail anyway.			
4. I made several good suggestions at the faculty committee meeting but no one seemed to pay any attention to them. It was as if I didn't say anything at all.			

WORKSHEET

Situation	Reflecting content response	Reflecting feelings response	Reflecting meanings response
5. I'm always blowing up at John. Later I realize there was little reason for it—what's wrong with me.			
6. The secretary always is interfering into my life. I wish she would mind her own business and get off my back.			
7. I'm having so much difficulty with Mary. She consistently arrives late for work.			
8. I wish Anne would stop borrowing my books. Every time I want to work on my paper, the books I want are not here.			

WORKSHEET

Situation	Reflecting content response	Reflecting feelings response	Reflecting meanings response
9. Our decision-making process isn't working. The people just don't follow the steps they should.			
10. My self-evaluation interview with my supervisor went well. I seem to be right on target with my personal goals.			
11. My wife nags at me from the moment I get home from work until I leave the house the next morning.			
12. My child doesn't seem to enjoy school. She comes home from school crying and says she doesn't want to go anymore. I'm at my wits end with this.			

WORKSHEET

Situation	Reflecting content response	Reflecting feelings response	Reflecting meanings response
13. My interview for the principal's job really went well. I think I'm sure to land the position.			
14. My children leave their clothes all over the house when they come home from school. They must think I'm a slave or something.			
15. The best teacher in my department informed me yesterday that she is pregnant and wants to stop teaching after the first of the year.			
16. Sometimes I get tired of doing make-up work with students who don't understand the concepts the first time around.			

EXAMPLE RESPONSES

Situation	Reflecting content response	Reflecting feelings response	Reflecting meanings response
1. These meetings continually last an hour or more over the allotted time, and I can't take that kind of time.	The meetings are really getting out of control for you.	You're feeling upset.	You feel upset when meetings last beyond the time scheduled.
2. I wish I were more accepted by the professor. I have a lot to contribute but just don't get called on much.	You're not as involved in class as much as you'd like.	You feel left out.	You feel dissatisfied when you're not invited to contribute.
3. I prepared and prepared for the exam next week. I just think I'm going to fail anyway.	Despite lots of preparation you're not expecting it to go well.	You're feeling frustrated.	You feel annoyed when your preparation doesn't seem to make any difference.
4. I made several good suggestions at the faculty committee meeting but no one seemed to pay any attention to them. It was as if I didn't say anything at all.	Your suggestions didn't seem to matter.	You're really feeling overlooked.	You feel discounted when no one pays attention to your ideas.
5. I'm always blowing up at John. Later I realize there was little reason for it—what's wrong with me.	—wondering if something is the matter with you.	You're feeling some concern.	You feel upset with your angry responses to John.
6. The secretary always is interfering into my life. I wish she would mind her own business and get off my back.	The secretary is a problem for you.	You feel irritated with her.	You're feeling upset about her interference.

EXAMPLE RESPONSES

Situation	Reflecting content response	Reflecting feelings response	Reflecting meanings response
7. I'm having so much difficulty with Mary. She consistently arrives late for work.	Mary's lateness is causing you some difficulty.	You're feeling displeased with her.	You feel upset when she comes in late for work.
8. I wish Anne would stop borrowing my books. Every time I want to work on my paper, the books I want are not here.	You don't have the books when you want them.	You feel frustrated.	You feel upset when Anne doesn't return your books.
9. Our decision-making process isn't working. The people just don't follow the steps they should.	They just aren't paying attention to details.	You're feeling irritated.	You're feeling upset about the lack of effectiveness in decision-making.
10. My self-evaluation interview with my supervisor went well. I seem to be right on target with my personal goals.	Things are going well for you.	You feel encouraged.	You feel good about accomplishing personal goals.
11. My wife nags at me from the moment I get home from work until I leave the house the next morning.	Your wife does a lot of complaining about you.	You're feeling angry.	You feel irritated because she complains so constantly.
12. My child doesn't seem to enjoy school. She comes home from school crying and says she doesn't want to go anymore. I'm at my wits end with this.	Your child is having problems at school.	You're feeling frustrated.	You're worried about your child's unhappiness at school.

41

EXAMPLE RESPONSES

Situation	Reflecting content response	Reflecting feelings response	Reflecting meanings response
13. My interview for the principal's job really went well. I think I'm sure to land the position.	The principal's job looks like a good possibility.	You feel confident.	You feel good about the interview and your job prospects.
14. My children leave their clothes all over the house when they come home from school. They must think I'm a slave or something.	—a lot of unnecessary work.	You're feeling abused.	You're angry that the kids don't seem appreciative of your needs.
15. The best teacher in my department informed me yesterday that she is pregnant and wants to stop teaching after the first of the year.	The teacher is going to leave.	You're feeling concerned.	You feel worried that you might be without a teacher.
16. Sometimes I get tired of doing make-up work with students who don't understand the concepts the first time around.	It's difficult to work with students who are having trouble.	You're feeling frustrated.	You feel overloaded with so much extra work.

Summarizing

Summarizing is listening accurately to another person and reflecting the main points of the other's communication in one to three sentences. The idea is to capture the essence of the other's thoughts and feelings about a particular value or perspective. For example, someone says to you:

> I think the arms race is one of the most stupid behaviors I've ever witnessed! We build 100 new missiles, so the Soviet Union builds 120; then we have to build another 50 to regain our advantage. This goes on and on, and the superpowers never seem to stop and see what they're doing. Both sides already have enough weapons to destroy each other's cities and production sites and to kill every person in the United States and the Soviet Union many times over. And we authorize expenditures for weapons that are often obsolete before they're ready for use. Besides that, we're wasting so much money on these idiotic weapons that we don't have enough to take care of human needs. I can't believe how the leader of our government and other governments can be so senseless!

A summary of the other's statement might be:

> You're upset and confused as to why government leaders would continue to escalate the arms race beyond security needs. The expenditures are often wasteful and take money away from important human needs.

The ability to summarize a significant part of a conversation or a person's entire view or perspective demonstrates accurate listening. This skill is essential in dealing with conflicts of values.

When to Use—and Not Use—Reflective Listening

The reflective listening process is facilitated when the following conditions are present:

- The other person has the stronger need to be heard and the greater emotional energy.
- You have, and choose to take, the time to listen.
- You feel reasonably accepting of the other.
- You can remain reasonably separate and objective and not become so personally involved in what the other is saying that you get triggered with a defensive response.
- You trust in the resources of the other person to be the expert in charge of his or her own life.

It is appropriate to leave the reflective listening process in the following circumstances:

- When no further use of the skills is required because the other has been heard.
- When sending an assertion message (see Chapter 6) to get your personal goals and needs met.
- When moving into conflict management (see Chapter 7).
- When facilitating the problem-solving process of another (see Chapter 5).
- When disclosing your own feelings.
- When providing additional information.
- When referring the person to someone else for assistance (see Chapter 5, section on Referral/ Transferral).

High-Risk Responses

A "high-risk"* response in reflective listening is a statement which is likely to take the focus off the other. Because a key element of listening is keeping the focus on the other's thoughts and feelings, a high-risk response is not an effective listening reflection. The communication process is often frustrated

*J. Gordon Myers, unpublished notes made available by author.

and blocked when the listener uses "high-risk responses." These responses are experienced by the other as interfering responses and are therefore particularly inappropriate when the other has a strong need, a problem, or is feeling high energy or pressure on an issue. High-risk responses generally fall into the following three categories:

1. *Sending solutions* is sidetracking the other person's communication by moving right away to a solution offered by you. Your questions, advice, ordering, threatening, moralizing, or logical arguments often interfere with the other person's exploring those thoughts and feelings that can lead to his or her own solutions which address the heart of the situation. Using responses in this category communicate the subtle message that "You're too dumb to figure this out so I will tell you."

2. *Evaluating* is changing the focus of the conversation by shifting it from the other's concerns to your own diagnosis, interpretation, judgment, or praise of the other person. The subtle message sent in this category is "There's something the matter with you."

3. *Withdrawing* is distracting the other person from his or her agenda, often by reassuring the other that everything will be all right or diverting to another agenda. The subtle message conveyed in this category is "I'm really uncomfortable hearing these feelings."

By taking the focus off the other, high-risk responses are very likely to:

- Derail the conversation.
- Block the other person from finding the solution to his or her problem.
- Lower the other person's self-esteem.
- Distance you from the other.
- Diminish the other person's motivation and initiative.

High-risk responses have the effect of decreasing contact with the other and blocking the other from saying more because they:

- Imply a desire to change or modify the other person.
- Take responsibility away from the other.
- Cause resentment or defensiveness.
- Carry hidden messages or implications.
- Are negative and therefore evoke a negative/aggressive response.

As shown in figure 12, the various high-risk responses can be grouped into three categories: sending solutions to the other, evaluating the other's words or actions, and withdrawing from the conversation. All these high-risk responses tend to take the focus off the other.

The following are some specific examples of typical high-risk responses:

SENDING SOLUTIONS:

1. *ORDERING*. Telling the other person to do something.

> You must do this.
>
> You can't do it.
>
> I expect you to do this.
>
> Stop it.
>
> Go apologize to her.

2. *THREATENING*. Telling the other person what negative consequences will occur if he or she does something; alluding to the use of force.

> You had better do this, or else!
>
> If you don't do it, then . . .

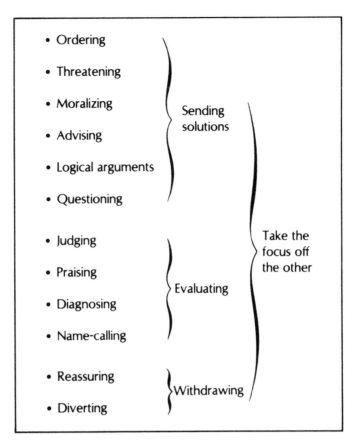

Figure 12. High-risk responses.

You'd better not try that.

I warn you, if you do that . . .

3. *MORALIZING.* Telling the other person why he or she ought to do whatever.

You really should do this.

You ought to try.

It's your responsibility to do this.

It's your duty.

I wish you would do this.

This is something I really urge you to do.

4. *ADVISING.* Telling the other person how to solve his or her problem.

What I think you should do is . . .

Let me suggest . . .

It would be best for you if . . .

Why not take a different approach?

If I were you, I'd . . .

The best solution is . . .

5. *LOGICAL ARGUMENTS*. Trying to influence the other person with facts, arguments, logic, information, or expert opinions that happen to agree with your own.

> Do you realize that. . .?
>
> The facts are in favor of . . .
>
> Let me give you the facts.
>
> Here is the right way.
>
> Experience tells us that . . .

6. *QUESTIONING*. Trying to find reasons, facts, motives, causes, information, etc., that will help you solve the other person's problem. (closed-ended questions.)

> Why did you do that?
>
> What have you done to solve it?
>
> Have you consulted anyone?
>
> Who has influenced you?

EVALUATING:

7. *JUDGING*. Making negative evaluations of the other person, agreeing or disagreeing with the other, or criticizing or blaming.

> You are acting foolishly.
>
> You're out of line.
>
> You didn't do it right.
>
> That's a stupid thing to say!
>
> I completely agree with you.
>
> You're absolutely right.
>
> You're all wrong on that point.
>
> I disagree.

8. *PRAISING*. Offering a positive evaluation or judgment (often condescending, sometimes sarcastic).

> Positively! (buttering up)
>
> You usually have such good judgment.
>
> You're an intelligent person.
>
> You have so much potential.
>
> You've made quite a bit of progress.
>
> You've always made it in the past.

9. *DIAGNOSING*. Telling the other person what his or her motives are or analyzing the "whys" behind what he or she is doing or saying. (Communicating that you have figured out, or diagnosed, the other.)

> You're saying this because you are angry.
>
> You are jealous.
>
> What you really need is . . .
>
> You have problems with authority.
>
> You want to look good.
>
> You're being a bit paranoid.

10. *NAME-CALLING.* Making the other person feel stupid, outcast, or foolish. (Stereotyping or categorizing.)

> You're a sloppy worker.
>
> You are a fuzzy thinker.
>
> You're talking like an engineer.
>
> You really goofed on this one!
>
> That was a dumb thing to do.

WITHDRAWING:

11. *REASSURING.* Trying to make the other person feel better; trying either to talk the other out of his or her feelings (making the feelings go away) or deny the strength of the feelings.

> You'll feel different tomorrow.
>
> Things will get better.
>
> It's always darkest before the dawn.
>
> Every cloud has a silver lining.
>
> It's not that bad.
>
> Don't worry so much about it.

12. *DIVERTING.* Trying to get the other person away from the problem or getting away from it yourself. Trying to change the focus by kidding, offering other things to do, pushing the problem away.

> Think about the positive side.
>
> Try not to worry about it until you've tried it.
>
> Let's have lunch and forget about it.
>
> That reminds me of the time when . . .
>
> You think *you've* got problems!*

---

*List of high-risk responses based on Thomas Gordon, *Parent Effectiveness Training* (New York: Wyden Publishing, 1970), pp. 41–44.

5

Problem Solving

Problem solving is a process of identifying a discrepancy between a current and a desired state and working out the steps required to reach that desired state. Figure 13 illustrates this definition graphically. Problem solving emerges in communication in three contexts:

1. Helping another with a problem when listening is not enough.
2. Resolving a difficulty you have with another.
3. Settling a dispute or difference between you and another.

In the first instance, the need to problem solve emerges when, in listening to another, you uncover that listening by itself is not enough. In the second instance you assert and find that the assertion process does not bring about your outcome—usually some indication of behavior change. In the third instance a conflict management strategy is indicated which requires working out a mutually agreeable solution. In all three cases, the generic problem solving process shown in figure 14 is applicable.

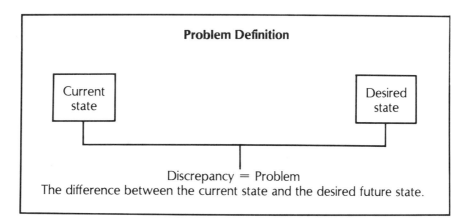

Figure 13. Problem definition.

Seven Step Problem Solving Process

1. Define problem in terms of desired state (result, needs).
2. Identify options for solution and clarify options that are ambiguous (brainstorm).
3. Evaluate alternative solutions.
4. Decide on an acceptable solution (one option or combination of options).
5. Develop an implementation/action plan (who will do what by whom).
6. Develop a process for evaluating the results (include in implementation/action plan).
7. Talk about the experience (of problem solving).

Figure 14. Seven step problem solving process.

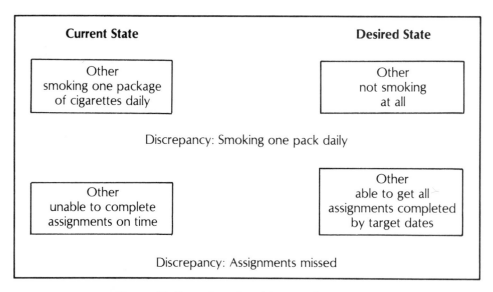

Current State	Desired State
Other smoking one package of cigarettes daily	Other not smoking at all

Discrepancy: Smoking one pack daily

Other unable to complete assignments on time	Other able to get all assignments completed by target dates

Discrepancy: Assignments missed

Figure 15. Examples of problem as discrepancy.

Two examples of discrepancies are shown in figure 15. In the first case the other wishes to move from a state of smoking cigarettes to a desired future state of non-smoking. The problem is the discrepancy, or the smoking behavior. In the second case the other wishes to get assignments completed on time. The discrepancy in this case is the work not done on time.

In the context of this chapter, the *Seven Step Problem Solving Process* is used to enable you to help another person who has a pressing need resolve a difficulty he or she is experiencing. However, not all pressing needs call for the use of problem solving skills; certain pressing needs call only for the use of reflective listening skills. The skills you use to help the other will therefore depend on your correctly identifying the other's needs or interests. The four types of situations you will encounter, together with the skills required to help the other deal with each type, are:

Type 1. *A pressing need that has no solution (for example, the death of a loved one).* Using reflective listening skills, you can provide a presence to the other as he or she copes with the situation. By listening acceptingly and supportively, you allow the other to explore and express the emotions he or she is experiencing.

Type 2. *A pressing need that is a problem that the other person has correctly identified and for which a solution is possible.* Using reflective listening skills you can commit to be with the other as he or she explains the problem. In talking the matter through, the other often clarifies the problem and is thereby helped to discover and move to his or her own solution.

Type 3. *A pressing need that is a concrete/specific problem that the other person has correctly identified and for which a solution is possible, but the other is unable to resolve the situation.* Using the problem solving skills presented in this chapter, you can facilitate the other's finding or developing his or her own solution.

Type 4. *A pressing need that is a broad/ambiguous problem which either is vague or a particular solution. A solution may be possible, but not until the problem has been clarified.* In this instance, problem clarification may be needed. The actual steps involved in the problem clarification process will be discussed in detail later in this chapter. In this case, more extensive reflective listening is necessary to clarify the problem before you can move into the problem solving process. The problem interview, used in the clarification process, helps the other move from a presenting problem that is unclear to a clarified problem that is specific and concrete.

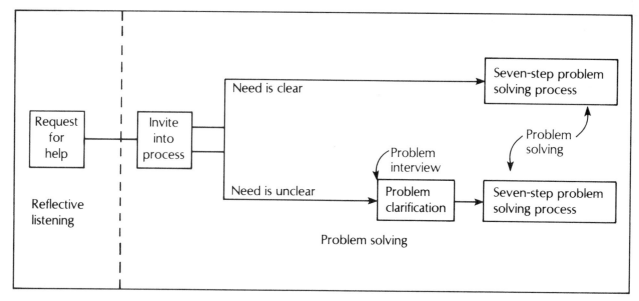

Figure 16. Entering the problem solving process.

Figure 16 illustrates how to enter the problem solving process with another, beginning with reflective listening to the pressing need presented by the other. If the pressing need has no solution (type 1) or if the person finds his or her own solution with your reflective listening (type 2) you do not have to enter problem solving at all. If a problem emerges (type 3 or 4) you would invite the other into problem solving using either the Seven Step Problem Solving Process (Figure 14) or the Problem Interview (Figure 17) to clarify the problem followed by the Seven Step Problem Solving Process. If the needs or interests of the other are clear and the presenting problem specific and concrete, you can move directly to problem solving. If the needs and interests of the other are vague, ambiguous or broad, the problem will need to be clarified (made more specific and concrete) using the problem interview.

Seven Step Problem Solving Process

The Seven Step Problem Solving Process, shown in Figure 14, is elaborated as follows:

Step 1: Define the problem

Define the problem in terms of the other's needs, as he/she expresses them in the reflective listening process. Asking the following questions is often helpful in helping another understand the discrepancy:

- What is the other's current state?
- What is the other's desired state or desired result expressed in terms of needs or interests? (Concrete behaviors, preferably see, hear, feel description of desired state.)
- What is the discrepancy between the two states?

Given that the problem is a discrepancy between a current state and a desired state, it is useful in problem solving to express the problem in terms of needs and interests underlying the desired future state, or result. This can be done by stating the problem as a "How to . . ." statement, using the following formula:

"How to _____ _____ ."
           (Action verb)   (Desired result)
                           Expressed in terms of
                           needs and interests.

Through reflective listening, you eventually reach the point where you can say, "It looks like we need to figure out "How to. . .". The statement will take the current state and the desired state into consideration but will be stated in terms of the desired state or result (where the other wants to get to). It must be a specific and practical statement which will clarify the discrepancy between the current state and the desired state. It is the first step in moving toward resolution of the discrepancy presented.

Examples:

"How to <u>   LEARN   </u>   <u>   REFLECTIVE LISTENING SKILLS   </u>."
                (Action verb)   (Desired result)

"How to <u>   LOSE   </u>   <u>   TEN POUNDS   </u>."
                (Action verb)   (Desired result)

"How to <u>   GET   </u>   <u>   A SALARY INCREASE OF $1.00 PER HOUR   </u>."
                (Action verb)   (Desired result)

Always try and make the "How to . . ." statement positive in nature, not negative.

For example:

NEGATIVE: "How to <u> STOP </u>   <u>   OVEREATING   </u>."

POSITIVE: "How to <u> EAT </u> <u>IN A WAY THAT MEETS YOUR NUTRITIONAL REQUIREMENTS AND MAINTAINS YOUR WEIGHT BETWEEN 120 AND 125 POUNDS.</u>

Another important aspect of the "How to . . ." statement is to make it as specific and concrete as possible. (See, hear, feel data.)

For example:

TOO GENERAL: "How to <u> LOSE </u>   <u> WEIGHT </u>."

MORE SPECIFIC: "How to <u> LOSE </u>   <u> TEN POUNDS </u>."

A third important aspect of the "How to . . ." statement is to be concise and to the point.

For example:

TOO LONG AND CONFUSING:

"How to <u>GET BACK ON THE RIGHT TRACK AND TRY AND START STUDYING SO I CAN FEEL CONFIDENT THAT I CAN PASS THIS COMMUNICATIONS COURSE, SO I'LL BE SURE TO GRADUATE IN MAY LIKE I HAVE BEEN PLANNING FOR FOUR YEARS.</u>

MORE CONCISE:

"How to <u> PASS </u>   <u> THIS COURSE </u>."

Step 2: Identify all possible options for a solution and clarify any options that may be ambiguous.

Once the problem is clearly defined, you can "brainstorm" to generate options that may resolve the discrepancy and enable the other to reach his or her desired state. It is very important that you involve the other in this brainstorming process as well as suggest anything you believe might be a possible solution. Be sure each of the possible options are clearly understood by both yourself and the other. It is useful to actually write the options on paper so that each of the parties can see as well as hear the list of possible solutions.

Step 3: Evaluate every option generated.

This step should be clearly separated from Step 2, in order that every option may be carefully considered. Combining steps 2 and 3 may cause a viable solution to be written off, before it is fully explored. It is also imperative that the other is involved in evaluating all the options. It is both more effective and respectful for you to help the other decide on his or her own solution, as opposed to giving the other the solution to the problem.

Step 4: Decide on an acceptable solution.

After full evaluation of each option, the other must decide which is best for him or her. There may be financial, time, lifestyle, or other variables that need to be considered before he or she make a decision. Only the other person knows which options are acceptable. The process is more effective when the person experiencing the problem decides on his or her own solution. If you provide the other with the answer to the problem, the likelihood of successful followthrough is diminished.

Step 5: Develop an implementation plan (action plan).

In this step, specificity is important. Now that an option or combination of options has been chosen, a number of things must be clearly specified, including:

- What are the steps needed to arrive at the solution?
- Who is responsible for each step?
- What resources are needed (i.e., money, time, etc.)?
- How long will it take (what is the target date for each step)?

It is also helpful to summarize what has been decided to ensure that every aspect of the solution has been carefully considered, and is clearly understood by the other.

Step 6: Develop a process for evaluating results.

This step involves building into the implementation plan a time and process for evaluating the results. Specific times must be set up to give the other an opportunity to talk about how the implementation plan is working. Such monitoring enables new problems to be addressed and any new variables considered. A final evaluation should take into account the entire effort.

Step 7: Talk about the experience.

After the implementation plan has been set up, you might invite the other to discuss his or her thoughts and feelings about the process, using some of the following questions as a guide:

- Does the other feel comfortable with the plan?
- Does the other understand all the aspects?
- How does the other feel about the problem solving process he or she has just gone through?
- Are there any questions?
- Is there anything you care to say before the meeting breaks up?

This last step in the problem solving process (talking about the experience) is important. A smooth close will encourage positive feelings in the other; an awkward close may stir negative feelings and reduce commitment to the implementation plan itself. It is important to summarize and to ensure the other that you will be available if any difficulties should arise if you have and are willing to take the time. Talking about the experience will hopefully bring out uncomfortable feelings and surface any remaining questions that might jeopardize the implementation plan. Always present yourself as caring, friendly, easy to talk to and helpful to the person in solving the problem.

This problem solving process develops an appropriate action plan for attending to the problem. Future steps would include implementing the solution and evaluating the results in accordance with the implementation or action plan.

The essence of the seven step problem solving process is allowing the other person to solve his or her own problem. It is both more effective and more respectful for the listener to help the other generate his or her own solution rather than to propose whatever solution might appear appropriate from the listener's viewpoint because:

- The other has more of the pertinent information about the problem: past, present and future.
- The other has to implement the solution, not you as the listener.
- The other takes all the risks.

- The other's self-confidence is fostered when he or she assumes responsibility for developing and implementing the solution.
- The other's feeling of independence is fostered when he or she takes responsibility for the problem, decides on an appropriate solution and implements the action plan.

Problem Clarification

The initial step when another presents a problem situation to you is to reflective listen. When you are convinced the other needs help then you can suggest problem solving or clarification, whichever seems to be appropriate. (Figure 16)

Often the other's need is ambiguous, or he or she cannot state it concretely. When this occurs, the Problem Interview, outlined in figure 17, is useful to clarify the problem. After the "How to . . ." statement has been agreed upon in a problem solving situation, you will need to check with the other to make sure you are an acceptable helper. There are two ways to invite another to use the seven step problem solving process:

The person asks for help—

Say: "I'd be glad to help you look at some options."

You sense the person wants help—

Ask: "Would you like me to help you look at some options?"

If the person's response is positive, describe the process as follows:

"A process that has been useful to me is to first identify the need, generate as many options as possible, and—if one seems to make sense—work out a plan to make it happen. How does that sound for you?"

In both problem clarification and problem solving:

1. *Do not lead the conversation.*
   Be sure to allow the other person to talk about his or her needs and perceptions of the problem. Let the other decide the direction of the conversation. Allow the other to bring up points he or she sees as important.

2. *Do not bombard the other with questions.*
   Asking too many questions is another way of diverting the conversation off the other's agenda. Although in problem clarification you will ask about the history of the problem, what has been tried so far and an ideal wish, you will not need to ask for names, dates, relationships, likes, dislikes, goals, etc. Closed-ended questions can easily turn into your interpretation and analysis of the problem being presented. It is important to remember that it is beneficial for the other to decide for himself or herself what the problem is and what plan of action to take. Another

---

Problem Interview

1. Explore the "problem as presented" with the other.
2. Paraphrase the "problem as presented" as a "how to ___" statement.
3. Invite the other to share the history of the problem.
4. Ask the other to share what has been tried so far.
5. Invite the other to identify his or her ideal result or wish.
6. Revisit the "problem as presented" and modify it as appropriate.
7. Invite the other to problem solve, if appropriate.

Figure 17. Problem interview. (Based on J. Gordon Myers, unpublished notes made available by the author.)

tendency is to ask a question to break an awkward moment of silence. Resist the temptation and remain silent. The other may be in deep thought and will continue talking when ready to formulate his or her thoughts into words. Many times interested silence can help the other continue in the direction of the conversation, or unearth a new thought and idea.

3. *Do not be judgmental.*

Important to building rapport and trust between you and the other is to be non-judgmental. If you find the other's problem distasteful or find yourself in an opposing value position and cannot disassociate yourself from it, you may choose not to be a helper in that specific situation. At all times try to be as objective and non-judgmental as possible.

4. *Do not offer your "advice."*

Again, it is important that the other decide what to do about his or her situation. It is almost natural to offer the kind of advice that says "What I'd do if I were you is . . ."; "What you need is . . ."; or "Let me tell you what I did in the exact situation". Avoiding giving advice keeps responsibility for the problem with the other. All of your best advice can be offered to the other in the form of an option to be considered.

Avoiding the "Don'ts" listed above will facilitate a good working relationship with the other—a relationship that will encourage the sharing of feelings and information, and one conducive to the successful resolution of the problem presented.

Referral/Transferral

As the problem or issue is defined and explored, and the other person wishes for or expects certain assistance from you, it may become apparent that his or her need is one that could more appropriately be dealt with by some trained individual or agency other than yourself. In such instances, you need to skillfully refer or transfer the person to whomever is capable of providing the needed assistance.

- *Referral* of a person involves broadening and sharing (not transferring) the responsibility for providing help. In referral you are not turning the person over to another party; you remain the person's primary support, but with another skilled party in collaboration.

- *Transferral* of a person involves taking steps to shift the responsibility for providing care and assistance from yourself to another skilled party.

The steps involved in referring or transferring a person whose need you cannot meet to another, more appropriate source of trained assistance are as follows:

1. Have a working knowledge of the resources available in the community. Think in terms of interprofessional cooperation (psychiatrists, psychologists, physicians, social workers, counselors, etc.) and develop the ability to pinpoint who is outside your professional world that you need inside it in a particular situation.

2. Hint at the possibility of referral/transferral early after discovering the need for such action.

3. Present the need for referral/transferral to the person with care, in a sensitive, reassuring way:
   a. Explain in detail what you perceive to be the person's need, based on what is emerging from the problem clarification interview or the problem solving process. Paraphrase and summarize the information the other has provided.
   b. Explain why you cannot meet the need.
   c. Explain the appropriateness of a particular person or agency that might be helpful.

4. Remain silent and allow the person to express his or her feelings, accepting these as genuine and crystalizing any problems that might arise from the person's adopting the recommended alternative approach (e.g., confidentiality, cost). Problem solve as appropriate.

5. Be understanding but firm.

6. Reassure the person that you are not stepping out of his or her life and clarify specifically how your relationship will continue. Expect him or her to feel rejected and respond to that rejection by helping the person get the hurtful feelings fully expressed and by letting the person know you have truly listened to those feelings.

7. To encourage initiative, follow up with the person, letting the other gauge the amount of follow-up required. However, leave the task of contacting the recommended third party up to the other.*

A basic insight is to accept referral/transferral as an integral part of the helping process, for no single individual can expect to provide a complete range of support that totally meets the needs of another person.

*Based on J. Gordon Myers, unpublished notes made available by the author.

6
Assertion

The skills of reflective listening and problem solving enable you to be present to other people and help them in situations of strong emotion. Assertion invites you to be present for yourself and to help you deal with your strong emotion. Assertion is essentially expressing yourself to stand up for your own human rights without infringing on the human rights of others. It is expressing your thoughts, feelings, opinions, and beliefs to another to achieve your outcomes without infringing on another, damaging your relationship with the other, or injuring his or her self-esteem. Assertion is basic to the communication process and essential for the development of interpersonal relationships.

In this definition, the word *right* refers to something to which you have some just and proper claim. A human right in the assertion context is anything that you consider all people are entitled to by virtue of their existence as human beings. Respect and care about one another as persons is an underlying premise. Some important human rights are:

- To be alone—to be by yourself.
- To be independent and maintain your separateness and individuality.
- To be competent and successful and to excel in whatever you choose.
- To be listened to with respect.
- To receive the product or services you have contracted for—to get what you paid for.
- To be assertive—to express yourself to meet your personal goals without infringing on another.
- To refuse requests and say no without feeling guilty or selfish.
- To request what you want from another.
- To make mistakes and be responsible for them.
- To choose not to confront another.*

While listening is a following posture, assertion is a leading, or initiating, posture. The essence of the distinction is as follows:

- In *listening* you are basically receiving from the other person. The material is the other's needs, thoughts, and feelings. Your task is to keep the focus on the person you are listening to. You are letting him or her impact you and come to you, while you respond. When you are listening, then, it is the other person who is taking all the risk and revealing himself or herself.
- In *assertion* the process flows in the other direction: you are the one who initiates. You go out of yourself to the other. The focus is on you—your needs, your thoughts, your feelings, your person. In assertion, then, you take the action, choose, and take the risk. You reveal yourself; your private self goes public.

Assertion requires a lot more energy and is personally more demanding than listening. Many people experience some anxiety when beginning to learn assertion skills. This is understandable, because assertion has its origin in your sense of self. As compared to listening, it is much more closely linked to how

*Based on Colleen Kelley, *Assertion Training: A Facilitators Guide* (San Diego, Calif.: University Associates, Inc., 1979), pp. 58–59.

you see yourself. It has to do with what you say to yourself about yourself, with your image of how others see you, and with your feelings about conflict. Assertion is an expression of whether you regard yourself as OK or not OK.

In order to assert well, you need a sense of your own worth, of power. You need to be centered and balanced. You need to see yourself as a person with choices—a person who owns and shapes his or her own life and is able to influence others.

Developing this sense of self is a life's work. In this learning experience, you will be able to increase your awareness of assertion as a life work, learn some skills and techniques that will facilitate growth, and become better able to apply assertion skills in your personal life.*

Personal Space

An understanding of the concept of personal space is useful in assertion. While people seem to have an innate sense of the physical and psychological space around them, needs for personal space differ:

- One person might be comfortable spending a lot of time in a room crowded with people, not minding a high noise level, jostling, many conversations at once, a lot of smoke. To another person, this could be anxiety-producing. He or she might be thinking: "I'm going right up the wall!"—a description of a frantic effort to escape and get more space.
- Some people don't mind being touched, while others feel invaded by uninvited touch, slaps on the back, nudges in line.
- Some people need a lot of privacy and alone time. Others want to be with people as much as possible.
- Some people are very uncomfortable and feel infringed on by a display of negative emotions in their presence. Others don't mind and can get right in on a good argument.

Much of your sense of personal space has to do with the culture and environment in which you were raised. The important realization is that we all have invisible boundaries, which means that when someone comes inside your space uninvited, you feel invaded in some way; when you go uninvited into someone else's, they generally feel transgressed upon. Consistently allowing someone to invade your space physically or psychologically is called *submission*. Invading another person's space is called *aggression*. In between the extremes of submission and aggression is the wide range of behaviors called *assertion*.

Figure 18 illustrates the concept of personal space. The large circle represents the area of personal space surrounding each individual (represented by the central dot). The boundary of the circle represents the point of assertion—that is, the point at which another person's behavior starts to impact the individual.

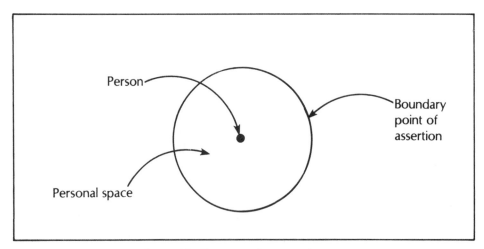

Figure 18. Concept of personal space.

*Based on John W. Lawyer and Patricia H. Livingston, *Communication Skills* (Pompey, N.Y.: Henneberry Hill Consultants, Inc., 1977).

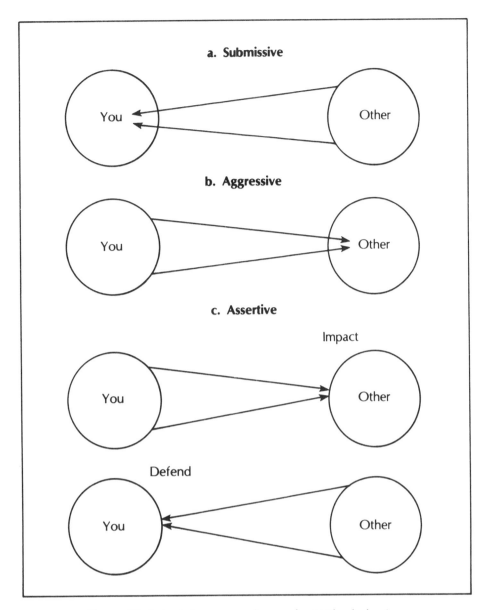

Figure 19. Submissive, aggressive, and assertive behavior.

Figure 19 illustrates the contrast between submission, aggression, and assertion. In figure 19a, "you" are allowing the "other" to infringe upon or invade your space, which is submissive behavior. In figure 19b, "you" are infringing on or invading the space of the "other," which is aggressive behavior. Figure 19c represents two types of assertive behavior. In the first, "you" impact the "other" with an appreciating assertion message; in the second, "you" defend yourself from infringement by the "other" by stopping the other's infringement at your boundary.

The range of behaviors related to personal boundaries can be pictured on the assertion continuum (see figure 20). At the far left of the continuum is submission—behaviors that allow the other to invade your space in some way. At the far right is aggression—behaviors in which you invade the other's space in some way. In between is the wide range of behaviors called assertion. Behaviors typical of persons who are habitually submissive, assertive, and aggressive are shown in figure 21.

Toward the right end of the assertion zone are behaviors in which you go out of yourself to the other. You do not invade the other's space, but you reach out to him or her in ways that impact, initiate, or influence. Examples of this kind of behavior would be teaching someone or sharing ideas, but without encroaching on the other's space. He or she is left free.

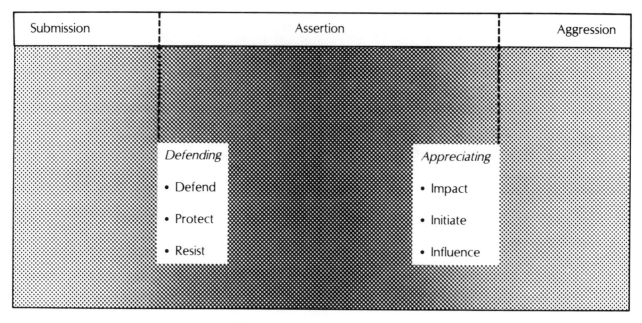

Figure 20. Assertion continuum.

Submissive	Assertive	Aggressive
Tendency to:	Tendency to:	Tendency to:
• Allow self to be interrupted, subordinated, and stereotyped	• State feelings, needs, and wants directly	• Interrupt, subordinate, and stereotype others
• Have poor eye contact	• Have good eye contact	• Have intense and glaring eye contact
• Have poor posture and defeated air	• Have straight posture and competent air	• Have invading posture and arrogant air
• Withhold information, opinions, and feelings	• Be able to disclose information, opinions, and feelings	• Conceal information, opinions, and feelings
• Be an ineffective listener	• Be an effective listener	• Be an ineffective listener
• Be indecisive	• Initiate and take clear positions	• Dominate
• Apologize, avoid, and leave	• Confront with skill	• Be loud, abusive, blaming, and sarcastic

Figure 21. Typical behaviors on the assertion continuum. (Based on Robert E. Alberti and Michael L. Emmons, *Stand Up, Speak Out, Talk Back!* [New York: Pocket Books, 1975], p. 39; and Colleen Kelley, *Assertion Training: A Facilitators Guide* [San Diego, Calif.: University Associates, Inc., 1979], p. 105.)

Most of you in this learning experience will find yourselves comfortable to some extent with the right, or appreciating, end of the assertion zone. This does not mean that there is no room for personal growth at this end of the continuum, since you can learn to relate to people better, to help others, to make suggestions more productively, to speak up more succinctly in meetings, and to influence others. You can also become less shy and get better at asking someone to spend time with you. As you come to feel more powerful, you will have more impact. Although you can grow more skillful in these areas, you probably will not have trouble with this aspect of assertion.

What you may have a lot more trouble with is the left, or defending, end of the assertion zone. This is the area in which you need defending skills, protecting skills, and resisting skills when conflict exists and someone is about to invade your space or is pushing against you. The situation in this case is already unpleasant to some extent, and skillful ways of behaving in these circumstances do not come so naturally.

In fact, while growing up, it is likely that most of you were richly rewarded for giving in, for not making waves, for not defending. For example: "You're such a good little girl; you never make a fuss." Or, "You're the boy who always gets along with everyone. I know I can count on you." In short, you may have been taught that it is selfish not to do what someone else wants you to do—selfish to object when someone is playing loud music when you are trying to sleep; "making a big thing out of nothing" to speak up when another person agrees with you to come to meetings and then repeatedly arrives late; "not being cooperative" when you resist being assigned another big project on top of your already packed schedule.

Because this aspect of assertion is more difficult for most of us, much of our time in this segment of the learning experience will be spent dealing with ways of defending, with ways of getting your personal goals and needs met. It is crucial, however, that in the process of getting your own needs met, you do not aggress against the other person. This learning experience will present ways to get your needs met that are also respectful of the other person—ways that have the least chance of lowering the other's self-esteem or damaging your relationship with him or her.

Choosing Behaviors

The essence of assertion is choosing. In assertion you experience yourself as a person of power. Your future does not just happen to you: you shape it with choices. You do not just respond automatically to an outside stimulus: you reflect on your experiences. In other words, you see yourself as having alternatives, and you choose how you wish to act.

It is helpful to visualize your response behavior as either "stimulus-response" or "stimulus-reflection-response" behavior, as shown in figure 22.

In *stimulus-response behavior,* a stimulus impacts you, and you react automatically. If the phone rings, you jump and answer it. If someone says he or she wants you to do something, you agree. If someone brings you food that is not what you ordered, you eat it anyway.

Much of our moral training encourages this kind of behavior. People have been taught exactly what to do in every circumstance, as if there were a prescribed way of behaving for every given situation. As a consequence, many people have remained immature, merely doing as they are told.

In *stimulus-reflection-response behavior,* a stimulus impacts you, and you reflect on a response before acting on it. You put yourself through a process of reflection before you act. *You choose.* This is assertive behavior. If the phone rings, you consider whether or not you want to allow the interruption at this time. If someone asks you to help with a project, you really think over whether or not you want that

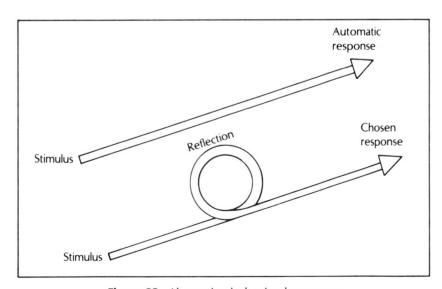

Figure 22. Alternative behavioral responses.

61

added responsibility. If a waitress brings your steak rare when you had ordered it well-done, you consider the matter and decide whether you want to accept and pay for what you did not order.

You may in fact think it over and choose to do the same thing you would have done if you had responded automatically. The point is that you have *chosen* to. The basic question in stimulus-reflection-response thinking is: which way of responding expresses how you most want to behave in this particular situation? In other words, the act of reflection and choice determines the assertiveness of a particular behavior. A response that might be viewed by another as submissive or aggressive might very well be assertive for you in a given situation as a consequence of your reflection and choice.

Table 2 provides an overview of submissive, assertive, and aggressive behaviors, comparing how the three types of behaviors affect the feelings both you and the other person have about the interaction.

Table 2. Feelings elicited by submissive, assertive, and aggressive behavior. (Adapted from Robert E. Alberti and Michael L. Emmons, *Stand Up, Speak Out, Talk Back!* [New York: Pocket Books, 1975], p. 39.)

	Submissive behavior	*Assertive behavior*	*Aggressive behavior*
Characteristics	Emotionally dishonest, indirect, self-denying, inhibited	(Appropriately) emotionally honest, direct, self-enhancing, expressive	(Inappropriately) emotionally honest, direct, self-enhancing at the expense of another, expressive
Your feelings when you engage in this behavior	Hurt, anxious at the time, and possibly angry later	Confident, self-respecting at the time and later	Righteous, superior, powerful at the time, and possibly guilty later
The other person's feelings about self when you engage in this behavior	Guilty or superior	Valued, respected	Hurt, humiliated
The other person's feelings about you when you engage in this behavior	Pity, irritation	Generally respect	Angry, vengeful

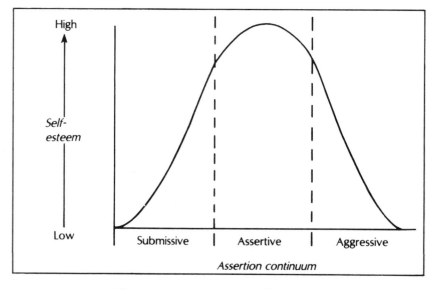

Figure 23. Assertion and self-esteem.

Assertiveness is related to self-esteem. Figure 23 illustrates the relationship between the level of assertiveness (assertion continuum) and self-esteem. People who habitually behave either submissively or aggressively generally have low self-esteem; people who are normally assertive have high self-esteem. The essential insight to be gained from this relationship is that when assertive skills are learned and practiced, self-esteem increases. Assertive people generally feel good about themselves.

Assertion Profile

With most individuals, assertion is situational. Under specific circumstances, or with a specific individual, you might choose to behave in typically submissive, aggressive, or assertive ways. Please use the Assertion Profile Worksheet to construct an assertion profile describing your typical response to different situations.

Assertion Profile Worksheet

Indicate a specific situation in each of the behavioral categories below. Record who you were with; where; what was happening; what you wanted to happen; what did happen; and what you felt, thought, and did. Then indicate the extent to which this example can be generalized—that is, the extent to which it typifies your behavior with respect to a particular person, a certain type of person, or a specific situation.

A time I behaved submissively:

A time I behaved assertively:

A time I behaved aggressively:

Some common themes that emerged for me:

Assertion Messages

The initial step in the assertion process is reflecting on the situation to develop clarity and then formulating an appropriate assertion message.

In developing assertion messages, it is useful to avoid messages which blame the other and helpful to use messages which insure that you take responsibility for your position in an assertion. These two types of messages are called "You messages" and "I messages." "You messages" put the focus on the other and blame the other, while "I messages" describe your needs and feelings and keep the focus on you. "You messages" are typically employed in unskillful attempts to get your needs met; "I messages," used in assertion, represent the skillful approach. For example, when someone cuts in front of you in line in the supermarket your response could be:

"You message"—

"You're incredibly rude cutting in front of me in line!"

"I message"—

"I believe I was next in line."

The following listing contrasts the two types of messages and shows the advantages of approaching assertion situations by focusing on the other's specific behavior, rather than trying to blame or judge the other.

"I messages"	versus	*"You messages"*
• Keep the focus on you		• Put the focus on the other
• Describe the behavior		• Seldom mention your needs
• Describe your feelings		• Seldom mention your feelings
• Are nonjudgmental		• Are blameful
• Are succinct		• Tend to be lengthy
• Are specific		• Are generalizations
• Foster the other's independence		• Foster dependence or counterdependence
• Tend to enhance the other's self-esteem		• Tend to lower the other's self-esteem

Assertion messages can take one of two forms—simple assertion messages or three-part assertion messages, which will be discussed in the following sections. Both simple and three-part assertion messages can be used either to express appreciation or to defend yourself from infringement:

- *Appreciating assertion messages*—used for appreciating, influencing, or affirming another or for initiating.
- *Defending assertion messages*—used for defending, protecting, or resisting infringement by another.

Simple Assertion Messages

A simple assertion message is a direct statement expressing yourself to get your needs met without infringing on the human rights of another. It can be used to protect yourself from infringement or to appreciate or affirm another.

Simple assertion messages usually involve an initial instance of infringement or positive behavior by another. In such cases, simple defending assertion messages can be used to protect you from the negative behavior of the other. Simple appreciating assertion messages can be used to affirm the other for behavior that has a positive effect on you. Examples might be:

I appreciate your returning my call so promptly.

I like it when you explain the directions so clearly.

I believe I also ordered a tossed salad.

My last name is Jackson, not Johnson.

Three-Part Assertion Messages

As its name implies, the three-part assertion message is a direct statement made up of three parts that is intended to get your needs met without infringing on the human rights of another. It is a description of the other person's behavior, its feeling effect on you, and the consequence for you. It is used to express appreciation for another or to protect yourself from infringement. It usually involves repeated behavior or a pattern of behavior. Examples might be:

When you always arrive on time for your appointment, I feel grateful because my next meeting can begin as scheduled.

When you are late for a meeting, I feel irritated because I need to take extra time to bring you up to date.

Three-part defending assertion messages are required for instances where infringements are repeated and a simple assertion message has not proved effective.

The general form of a three-part assertion message is as follows:

"When you _____ I feel _____ because _____ ."

1. "When you _____ . . ."
   (Concrete description of the other's behavior.)

2. ". . . I feel _____ . . ."
   (Appropriate, accurate disclosure of your feeling about the other's behavior.)

3. ". . . because _____ ."
   (Description of the concrete and tangible effect of the other's behavior on you.)

A three-part message is used when the assertion involves some concrete effect on the person asserting, such as time, property, money, or health. Because the three-part message involves physical space, all three parts of the message are appropriate.

Sometimes assertion messages can consist of only two parts. When the message involves the other person's decisions, beliefs, moods, values, preferences, life-style, or feelings—that is, when it involves an intangible effect—only the first two parts of the three-part message indicated above are normally used.

Self-Disclosure

Both defending and appreciating assertion messages essentially involve self-disclosure. Self-disclosure is revealing to another what is happening within yourself at the moment. Its purpose is to establish and build relationships or defend yourself against infringement.

Appropriate criteria for self-disclosure are listed below, with each criterion followed by an *A* and/ or a *D* to indicate whether the criterion applies to appreciating assertion messages, defending assertion messages, or both.

1. *Goal-directedness.* You should understand clearly why the disclosure is being made.　　A　　D

2. *An eye to proportion.* The amount of self-disclosure should be proportional to the goal.　　A　　D

3. *Respect and caring.* There should be basic respect for the other person.　　A　　D

4. *Ongoing quality of the relationship.* The desire for continuity with the other person should be clear. A D

5. *Mutuality.* When mutuality does not exist, then self-disclosure is normally inappropriate. But this is not to imply that when mutuality does exist self-disclosure should be a tit-for-tat game, a kind of mindless exchange of intimacies. Self-disclosure is characterized by freely given statements about self. A

6. *Timing.* Self-disclosure should emerge from and relate to what is happening at the moment or to a specific behavior in the recent past. A D

7. *Here and now.* Self-disclosure should deal with the here and now or in some way be related to the here and now. This means that if your self-disclosure message concerns matters from the past, you should take pains to relate what you are talking about to what is happening with the other at the moment. A D

8. *Gradual.* Relationships are built gradually; what is revealed should not drastically change or restructure relationships. A

9. *Risk.* Taking the risk of expressing your feelings creates a climate of trust. Self-disclosure is a way of entrusting yourself to another. A

10. *Impact.* Self-disclosure should be judged for its impact on the other. If it is too intimate, the message should be tempered and made more gradual. A

11. *Shared context.* Self-disclosure is appropriate when the individuals involved are sharing the same goal or working on the same problem—i.e., when there is enough in common to sustain the disclosure. A

12. *Response to self-disclosure.* By their nature, self-disclosure messages demand some type of response. The most appropriate response is an indication from the listener that the self-disclosure message has been heard and received acceptingly. Reflective listening skills presented in this learning experience provide the basis for an appropriate kind of response.* A D

Assertion Sequence

Assertion fundamentally involves choice, where you choose a behavior appropriate to a particular situation. In a specific instance you may choose to act in a way that appears to be aggressive or submissive, and the behavior is assertive because it is chosen. If the behavior is an automatic response, however, it may well be submissive or aggressive.

Although assertion messages can be used to defend yourself against infringement or express appreciation for behavior that has had a positive effect on you, most of the time they are used to invite another to modify infringing behavior. The three-part assertion message, described in greater detail in the next section, is often called a "behavior-change message." The assertion sequence, described in this section, is a process that invites behavior change and is used in defending situations.

Whenever you are infringed on, you have five choices. You can:

1. *Be aggressive*—confront the other without the use of skills, thereby infringing on the other in return. For example, you are just falling asleep, and someone in the adjacent, interconnecting hotel room turns the television on loud. You might then beat on the interconnecting door, yelling "Turn that TV down!"

2. *Modify yourself*—choose to meditate or quiet yourself and hope you can transcend the effects of the infringement. In the case of the example, you might grit your teeth and count sheep.

3. *Modify the environment*—change the immediate surroundings in some way so as to lessen the effects of the infringement. In the example, you might hang a blanket over the interconnecting door and stuff a pillow under the door.

*Based on Gerard Eagan, *The Skilled Helper* (Monterey, Calif.: Brooks/Cole, 1975), pp. 127–56.

4. *Withdraw or be submissive*—remove yourself from the environment and find one more suitable to your needs. In the example, you might call the desk, complaining about the situation, and ask that you be transferred to another room.

5. *Assert with skill*—use the assertion skills presented in this learning experience to bring about a change in the other's behavior. In the example, you might go to the door of the adjacent room, knock, and when the other answers, ask, "Please turn the television down. The noise is interfering with my sleep."

The *assert with skill* choice, emphasized in this learning experience, presumes the use of the assertion sequence. The sequence is a process for assertion in situations where you have a positive, relatively strong relationship with the other. This process is built on a basis of trust developed by being fair; treating the other with respect; being honest, open, and direct; and listening with skill. There are five stages in the assertion sequence:

Stage 1. *Expectations and Standards.*
   The *clear communication of expectations,* which can include agreements, contracts, standards, policies, procedures, rules, or understandings.
   If infringement occurs or a problem arises, then conduct:

Stage 2. *Monitoring.*
   a. The initial assertion, using a simple assertion message to point out specifically any problem area or area of infringement. This is an opportunity to also repair any loopholes in the original agreement.
   If infringement occurs or a problem arises again, then conduct:
   b. The *reminder conversation,* using a simple assertion message to point out specifically the continuing infringement and clarify the standard or prior agreement about behavior. This conversation can serve to clarify any misunderstandings and provide you with the opportunity to offer help.
   If infringement occurs or a problem arises again, then hold:

Stage 3. *Initial Confrontation Meeting.*
   The *confrontation meeting,* reviewing the history of the problem and using the three-part assertion message to work out an agreement that meets your needs. If the assertion message doesn't bring about agreement, utilize conflict-management and problem solving strategies (see Chapter 7) to attempt resolution. Either process should result in a renewal of the contract or agreement or a new contract, agreement, or action plan to ensure resolution of the difficulty.
   If infringement or problem persists, then hold:

Stage 4. *Second Confrontation Meeting.*
   At the second confrontation meeting, you confront the broken agreement that was approved in Stage 3 stating the consequences if the behavior doesn't change and giving the other time to decide on whether or not he or she can accept the situation.
   If the problem behavior persists, activate the consequences and move to activate the consequences and move to:

Stage 5. *The decision meeting,* communicating to the person the need to examine the relationship itself and indicating that if the behavior continues to persist, the relationship will need to be modified or terminated—e.g., a person working for you will need to explore the possibility of a job change; a close friend will need to change the nature of his or her relationship with you; or an associate will need to consider terminating your professional relationship.*

---

*Adapted from Ed Lisbe, *Assertion Messages* (unpublished manuscript made available by the author, 1980); used with permission.

Most infringements or problems can typically be corrected by assertive behavior using this sequence. In relationships built on mutuality and trust, the person is likely to modify his or her behavior before the third step, the initial confrontation meeting.

Message Formulation

Although both defending and appreciating assertion messages are dealt with in this section, the emphasis is on the formulation of defending assertion messages used to invite behavior change. In the first three subsections, the focus is on the accurate description of each of the parts of an assertion message. Defending messages are used in these sections because most often assertion involves inviting another who is infringing you to alter his or her behavior. The same format can be used in appreciating assertion to eliminate what is called judgmental praise, identified as a high-risk response in Chapter 3. In the fourth subsection, Assembling Three-Part Assertion Messages, both defending and appreciating assertion messages are considered.

While there are several ways of confronting problem behavior, three-part assertion messages are particularly effective in dealing with persistent problems—those behaviors that continue after several attempts have been made to change them. Well-prepared and skillfully delivered assertion messages can motivate others to voluntarily change their behavior without spending time in unnecessary arguments.

As indicated earlier, three-part assertion messages consist of a description of:

- The problem behavior pattern.
- Your feeling about the situation.
- The concrete and tangible negative effect of that pattern of behavior on your life.

The three parts are stated as briefly as possible and combined in one sentence, as follows:

When you *(problem behavior pattern)* . . .

I feel *(your feeling)* . . .

because *(negative effect on your life)*.

This structured format helps ensure that all three parts of the message are included. As you gain experience with this method of confronting others, you will be able to develop a style that is more natural for you and will convey the three necessary pieces of information in an integrated way.

Often the phrase "as we agreed" can be added to the first part of the message to refer to the contract or agreement developed between you and another in a prior conversation. When used, it need only be stated during the first time the assertion message is sent to the other.

The following sections present guidelines and exercises to help you develop your ability to formulate each of the components of a three-part assertion message.*

Describing the Behavior

When another's behavior has a negative effect on your life, one of the three things you need to communicate is a description of the behavior that is causing you a problem. Even when a person wants to meet your needs, it is unlikely that he or she will change a behavior that is bothersome to you unless he or she knows exactly what is going on that troubles you.

In developing this "behavior" component of the three-part assertion message, the following guidelines are helpful:

1. Describe the behavior accurately (specify what you are seeing or hearing).
2. Include any agreements.
3. Include a brief example.

*The following guidelines and exercises adapted from Ed Lisbe, *Assertion Messages* (unpublished manuscript made available by the author, 1980); used with permission.

4. Specify the right behavior.

5. Describe the pattern of behavior.

6. Avoid using inflammatory words.

7. Avoid using generalizations.

8. Avoid using adjectives.

9. Don't use adverbs.

These guidelines are elaborated below in short subsections, each of which presents a multiple-choice exercise, followed by a brief discussion of the most appropriate response and the inappropriate responses for the exercise. An understanding of the guidelines will enable you to formulate the first part of a three-part assertion message more effectively.

Describe the Behavior Accurately

Describing behavior is a difficult skill. Behavior is a person's actions—what he or she says or does. It is objective—what would be seen or heard. But people tend to describe "behavior" subjectively, from their own perspective—that is, they tend to interpret behavior, focusing on what they think the behavior meant rather than on what they saw or heard. When they do that, it is *not* a description of behavior. For example, one person might see another taking paper home from the office and "describe" that action as cheating the organization. That is a personal, subjective interpretation of what happened. The behavior actually known to be involved is that of "taking paper from the office." That is the behavior you saw. To attach your interpretation of the meaning of what a person does increases the likelihood that there will be a misunderstanding when you confront him or her.

Please read the following situation and select the best response.

Situation: You are the principal of a small private school. You have agreed to share decision-making with your staff whenever an issue concerns them. One member, Sylvia Rossin, has absented herself from the weekly staff meeting several times, and thus has not contributed to the decision-making process. Yesterday afternoon she was absent again. Because you value her presence in the staff meeting, you decide to confront her.

Question: Which of the following statements best describes Sylvia Rossin's behavior?

_____ a. "When you don't carry your share of the load in the staff meeting . . ."

_____ b. "When you don't attend staff meetings . . ."

_____ c. "When you disregard the needs of the staff . . ."

Responses:

b. (Most Appropriate) The behavior was that Sylvia Rossin did not attend the staff meetings. This is the description of the actual behavior.

a. (Inappropriate) From the data in the example you don't know whether or not Sylvia is doing an appropriate percentage of the workload ("carrying the load"). The behavior you are trying to change is her not attending the staff meetings.

c. (Inappropriate) Sylvia might not have been "disregarding" the needs of the staff at all. One of the reasons she might not have attended was because she was busy with duties. Guessing someone else's motivation can lead to a needless argument. The behavior to be changed here is that of not attending the staff meetings.

Include Any Agreements

People usually react defensively when someone confronts them about misbehavior. This defensive reaction (i.e., "I didn't do it") is natural and can therefore be expected. One way to diminish this natural defensive tendency is to mention a prior agreement that the person made with you about the problem behavior.

To include the agreement, you can add the phrase "as we agreed" or something similar to the assertion message. This will probably help the other recognize the facts of the situation more quickly.

Please read the following situation and select the best response.

Situation: You are the principal of a small private school. You have agreed to share decision-making with your managers whenever an issue concerns them. One member, Sylvia Rossin, has absented herself from the weekly staff meeting several times, and thus has not contributed to the decision-making process. Yesterday afternoon she was absent again. Because you value her presence in the staff meetings, you decide to confront her.

Question: Which of the following statements best describes Sylvia Rossin's behavior?

_____ a. "When you don't attend weekly staff meetings . . ."
_____ b. "When you don't follow our agreement about attending staff meetings . . ."
_____ c. "When you don't attend weekly staff meetings, as we agreed . . ."

Responses:

c. (Most appropriate) The behavior is described accurately and the agreement about attending the staff meetings is included.

a. (Inappropriate) This is a good description of the behavior and it would probably work for you if you asserted with it. By not mentioning the agreement you made, you might have to spend more time dealing with this person's defensive reaction to you.

b. (Inappropriate) Although your agreement was mentioned here, it is not the infringing behavior. The infringement is not attending staff meetings. An assertion has a greater chance of working if the specifics of the desired behavior are included in the message.

Include a Brief Example

Another way to help diminish the other person's defensiveness is to give an example of the kind of problem behavior you are talking about. Specific examples will help keep the situation being discussed in a clear perspective.

Some ways to include examples are:

". . . such as this morning when . . ."
". . . for example, the situation with Fred yesterday."

Please read the following situation and select the best responses.

Situation: You are the principal of a small private school. You have agreed to share decision-making with your staff whenever an issue concerns them. One member, Sylvia Rossin, has absented herself from the weekly staff meetings several times, and thus has not contributed to the decision-making process. Yesterday afternoon she was absent again. Because you value her presence in the staff, you decide to confront her.

Question: Which of the following statements best describes your associate's behavior?

_____ a. "When you don't attend weekly staff meetings as we agreed, like yesterday . . ."
_____ b. "When you didn't attend the staff meeting yesterday as we agreed . . ."
_____ c. "When you don't attend weekly staff meetings as we agreed . . ."

Responses:

a. (Most Appropriate) This message includes a description of the behavior you want changed, the agreement you made about the behavior and an example of the behavior.

c. (Inappropriate) This is a good description of the problem behavior and it includes the agreement that was made. It does not illustrate the point with an example, something that can improve the effectiveness of the message.

b. (Inappropriate) It is not just yesterday's meeting that is the problem. This is only one example of a behavior that has happened before. The overall behavior pattern should be stated first, with a specific instance (in this case, yesterday) added afterwards.

Specify the Right Behavior

If you assert to someone about the wrong behavior—that is, if you are imprecise and assert about behavior other than that which is actually bothering you—the problem will not be solved. Surprisingly, this happens quite often, partly because people tend not to speak clearly when confronting others. In addition, problem situations are not always easily described, and it may be difficult to pinpoint the specific problem-causing behavior.

Please read the following situation and select the best response.

Situation: As a student you are required to have the addition of a class to your schedule approved by your faculty advisor. You are upset with Dr. Skobac, your adviser, over the amount of time it is taking him to respond to your request for an additional art class. Because of the delay, the class may be filled, and you will be out of luck. According to agreements, these responses should come within a couple of days.

Question: Which of the following is the preferred way of describing Dr. Skobac's behavior that bothers you.

_____ a. "When you don't approve my request for an additional class . . ."

_____ b. "When you don't approve my request for an additional class within a couple of days, as the agreement states . . ."

_____ c. "When you don't tell me within a couple of days whether or not my additional class has been approved . . ."

Responses:

c. (Most Appropriate) This message lets Dr. Skobac know that you are having problems with the delay, not with whether or not the additional class gets approved.

b. (Inappropriate) You want an answer within a couple of days. Approval would be nice, but the answer is what you are after with this assertion. This statement puts a pressure on Dr. Skobac that you are not intending and is not likely to get you what you really want.

a. (Inappropriate) Once again you want an answer within a couple of days. Approval would be nice, but the answer is what you are after with this assertion. This statement also puts a pressure on Dr. Skobac that you are not intending and is not likely to get you what you really want.

Describe the Pattern of Behavior

It is rarely useful to correct only one problem in a series of similar behaviors. You might get the change you want in the specific instance, but other identical problems might continue. For example, suppose you are upset about a peer's behavior pattern of usually starting meetings late. Today he began half an hour late, and you could have used that time to accomplish other tasks. Hoping to change his behavior, you make an appointment to see him. Early in the conversation you tell him:

"Fred, when you *start your meetings 30 minutes late* . . ."

After some talking, Fred assures you that it won't happen again. Three weeks later, the meeting begins 18 minutes late. Fred thinks he has met your need (since he didn't start *as* late), but you remain frustrated. You still have nearly the same problem you had originally. You got the behavior change you *requested,* but not the one you really *wanted.* To accomplish your purpose, you would address the pattern of behavior, using the 30-minute situation, such as:

> "Fred, when you *start your meetings after the scheduled time,* such as this morning, when you began 30 minutes late . . ."

Please read the following situation and select the best response.

Situation: Though you've discussed filing mistakes with your secretary, she still misplaces your folders. Last night, when you stayed late in the office to finish a report, it took forty-five minutes to locate one of your patient's (Mr. Peter Ames) personnel folder because it was misfiled. You found it filed in the H's. You are feeling very upset about the loss of time. You decide to confront your secretary the following morning to insure that this behavior doesn't happen again.

Question: What message would be most likely to correct the problem behavior?

_____ a. "When you file Mr. Ames' records under 'H' instead of 'A' . . ."

_____ b. "When you don't file Mr. Ames' record where it belongs . . ."

_____ c. "When you don't file material where it belongs, such as putting Mr. Ames' personnel folder under 'H' . . ."

Responses:

c. (Most Appropriate) This message refers to the overall behavior pattern of which Mr. Ames' folder is a part.

a. (Inappropriate) If this message works, and your secretary agreed to change her behavior, all you can be sure of is that Mr. Ames' record will no longer be filed under 'H'. Other misfilings might continue.

b. (Inappropriate) If this behavior change occurs, you are only assured that Mr. Ames' record will always be filed correctly. Your problem is with other misfilings as well.

Avoid Using Inflammatory Words

Inflammatory words used in an assertion message often trigger an emotional reaction in the person asserted to. If you say "When you *failed* to do . . .," the person you are talking with will probably focus on a different meaning of the word *fail* than the one you intended. The other might experience a higher emotional response around the word *fail* than is desirable. This high-energy response blocks his or her ability to really understand what you are saying and respond constructively to it.

"When you *neglect* to inform me about . . ." is another example of usage of an inflammatory word. To avoid using words such as *failed* or *neglected* simply substitute the words *don't* or *didn't.*

Profane words are highly inflammatory for many people and, thus, are to be avoided in an assertion statement.

Please read the following situation and select the best response.

Situation: You have just moved to a new city. When the brakes went out on your car, a neighbor recommended a repair shop. You had the car fixed at "Roy's Repair Shop", and within sixty days the pads and rotors needed replacement, due to faulty reconstruction. You are upset with George, the mechanic who worked on your car, because he did not follow established procedures for brake replacement, and now you have to pay. You want to change his behavior.

Question: How can you best phrase a description of George's behavior?

_____ a. "When you ignore procedures, such as not having your work checked when you have finished . . ."

_____ b. "When you don't follow procedures about replacement of brakes by not having your work checked when you are finished . . ."

_____ c. "When you neglect procedures about brake replacement by not having your work checked when you are finished . . ."

Responses:

b. (Most Appropriate) This message has none of the "loaded" words that tend to increase a person's tension. With this approach, you are more likely to get George to understand what you are saying about his behavior.

a. (Inappropriate) The word "ignore" tends to make people very defensive. They are likely to respond to your statement by saying, " 'Ignore?' What do you mean 'ignore'? I meant to do it, I just. . . ." Their energy becomes focused on the word "ignore", rather than on the message you want them to hear.

c. (Inappropriate) "Neglect" is one of those words that triggers people emotionally. It implies not only that they didn't do something, but also that their error was somehow purposeful.

Avoid Using Generalizations

The words *always, never,* and *constantly* are generalizations and imply that there are no exceptions to what you are saying. Generalizations are rarely true—especially when you are talking about someone's behavior. Few people are "always" late for work. There are usually some occasions when they arrive on time, although it might not seem so when they are frequently late. Using an absolute will probably be detrimental to your assertion. The other person is likely to argue with you about the few occasions when he or she was on time, rather than focus on your concern for the times the behavior caused you a problem.

Please read the following situation and select the best response.

Situation: Milton, your best friend, borrows your philosophy notes for study to supplement his own. He always promises to return them the day he uses them, but occasionally forgets. Yesterday he borrowed your notes and didn't return them, and you need them for class. This is the third time this has occurred, and you are very upset.

Question: Which of the following messages is preferred in terms of changing Milton's behavior?

_____ a. "When you constantly borrow my notes and don't return them . . ."
_____ b. "When you don't return the notes you borrow, as we agreed, like my philosophy notes yesterday . . ."
_____ c. "When you never bother to return my notes . . ."

Responses:

b. (Most Appropriate) This message describes the behavior without exaggerating the number of times it has occurred.

c. (Inappropriate) The word "never" is not needed. Milton has probably returned the notes at least once in the past year. He will probably talk about the few times he returned the notes rather than hear your legitimate concern.

a. (Inappropriate) The word "constantly" is not accurate and using it will not help you to get Milton to change his behavior. Milton has probably returned the notes at least once in the past year so he will tend to argue until he proves that you are wrong to say "constantly". In addition to being in-accurate, the use of the word "constantly" will tend to increase Milton's defensiveness and make it more difficult for you to get the content of your message across.

Avoid Using Adjectives

It is important to be as specific as possible in describing behavior. Adjectives are not specific and should therefore be avoided. Adjectives tend to lead to arguments about "how long is long?" or "how short is short?" To tell a person she "takes extended breaks" or "schedules long meetings" or "submits

73

inaccurate reports" does not give her the kind of information she needs to change her behavior. "Long" can mean twenty minutes to one person and two hours to another. Rather than saying "When you take extended coffee breaks . . .," it would be more specific to say "When you take more than the agreed upon fifteen minutes for coffee breaks. . . ."

Please read the following situation and select the best response.

Situation: On several occasions Lois has received telephone messages for you and has conveyed the message inaccurately, either with the wrong name, or the wrong telephone number. This has resulted in your being unable to return the call to the person, which has embarrassed you. You are upset with Lois and decide to assert to her.

Question: Which of the following best tells Lois about the behavior that needs to be changed?

_____ a. "When you make flagrant mistakes in my telephone messages . . ."

_____ b. "When you give me inaccurate and incomplete phone messages . . ."

_____ c. "When you don't convey telephone messages to me accurately, like this morning's call with the wrong phone number . . ."

Responses:

c. (Most Appropriate) You told Lois the exact part of her behavior that was causing you a problem. You describe the data you were not getting accurately, i.e., the phone number in the telephone message this morning.

a. (Inappropriate) Since Lois gives you phone messages and names, addresses and phone numbers, she doesn't understand what is not "right" about the information. You probably think she knows what you mean, but your lack of clarity makes it difficult for Lois to know what you want.

b. (Inappropriate) Lois doesn't know what is inaccurate about the information she gives you. In fact, she probably believes it is accurate. Further, she will probably become more defensive than necessary, making it difficult for you to resolve the problem.

Don't Use Adverbs

When confronting another, it is usually not helpful for you to focus on the number of times the problem behavior has occurred in the past. The words *frequently, often, repeatedly,* or *regularly* in an assertion message aggravate your problem with the other in two ways:

1. The words tend to add blame to the message, because the focus becomes more on the past history than on the current behavior.

2. The words open the door to unnecessary arguments, such as "How often is often?"—the same problem that occurs with the use of absolutes and adjectives.

Please read the following situation and select the best response.

Situation: Your father has agreed to take a walk on the beach with you. You wanted this occasion to tell him about some of the difficulties you are having with school. He has scheduled this meeting two times and has cancelled at the last minute both times, and you are feeling annoyed.

Question: Which statement would probably be least likely to increase your father's defensiveness and be most likely to make him receptive to your assertion?

_____ a. "When you cancel appointments at the last minute, as with our appointment for a walk this morning . . ."

_____ b. "When you repeatedly promise to walk with me, and cancel at the last minute, like this morning . . ."

_____ c. "When you consistently avoid meeting with me, like this morning . . ."

Responses:

a. (Most Appropriate) You have used no words to make your father feel blamed. You want to achieve change for the future and realize that references to the past is not likely to achieve that purpose. By not reminding your father of the frequency of the problem at this point, your chances of getting him to listen and to understand are increased.

b. (Inappropriate) This is a pretty good message. The one word, repeatedly, if deleted, would clean up the message. This is because such words are often received as a form of blame and this increases defensiveness unnecessarily.

c. (Inappropriate) With the deletion of the word "consistently" this message is satisfactory. Again, consistently can be perceived by the other as a blaming word.

Describing Your Feelings

The second part of the three-part assertion message is a description of the feeling effect on you. It is a feeling word that captures your level of emotion about the problem behavior and its effect on your life. The lists of feelings words included in the Appendix can help you select an appropriate word to represent a particular feeling.

In developing the "feeling" component of the three-part assertion message, the following guidelines are helpful:

1. Use a feeling word that accurately describes how you feel.
2. Don't use the same word to describe all your feelings.
3. Don't use stronger feelings to build your case.
4. Don't use "victim" words.

Each of these guidelines is elaborated below. The multiple-choice exercises provided in the subsections covering the guidelines are followed by brief discussions of the most appropriate response and the inappropriate responses for each exercise.

Use a Feeling Word That Accurately Describes How You Feel

Describing your feelings in a three-part assertion message is an effective way to convey to the other person the importance of what you are saying. A major consideration when choosing a feeling word is to be sure it appropriately captures your level of emotion about the infringing behavior. For example, you could be furious about the same behavior that would only irritate someone else. The feeling word is unique for each person who is infringed by another.

Please read the following situation and select the best response.

Situation: Carrie doesn't think she should be as upset as she is about Rachel's disorganization in the apartment, because she is such an outstanding roommate in other respects. What bothers her most about the disorder is that Rachel herself doesn't know where things are when they need to locate things. She ends up sorting through drawer after drawer for a needed item. This takes a great deal more time than it would if she helped keep the apartment organized. They talked about this behavior before, but it seems that Rachel is just one of those non-detail oriented people. Carrie is considering talking to her again, but doesn't know the "best" approach regarding how much of her feelings to express—especially because she doesn't want to turn off such a good roommate.

Question: What would be the most appropriate feeling for Carrie to add to this message?

_____ a. ". . . I feel somewhat upset."

_____ b. ". . . I really feel frustrated."

_____ c. ". . . it bothers me a little."

Responses:

b. (Most Appropriate) This is probably close to what Carrie is feeling. If Rachel has persisted in her behavior, despite Carrie's previous attempts at talking with her, she needs to know the strength of her feeling. This understanding will help to make her more receptive to changing her problem behavior.

a. (Inappropriate) Carrie is more than "somewhat upset". Worse, her feelings of resentment seem to be building. If she doesn't let Rachel know her genuine feelings, the fine living relationship they now have will probably deteriorate.

c. (Inappropriate) Tempering her approach in this way, so as not to turn Rachel off, can only lead her to one conclusion: "She must not be too upset about this." Carrie needs to let her know that she is not liking this one particular behavior. If, given the overall perspective of her excellent behavior she wasn't bothered, she wouldn't need to say anything.

Don't Use the Same Word to Describe All Your Feelings

For many people, feelings are limited to such words as *good, bad, happy,* and *sad.* The range of anger words, from *upset* and *irritated* to *furious* and *irate,* usually all end up as "I'm angry". The word *frustrated* also tends to cover several levels of feeling.

It helps another believe that your life is negatively affected by his or her behavior if you can label the real feeling it causes in you.

Please read the following situation and select the best response.

Situation: One of your students has an excellent mind and contributes much to the class. There is one problem that concerns you with this person. She is erratic in meeting deadlines. She will be on time for several assignments, then, with no warning, she will miss a deadline and appears to think that doesn't matter. It creates an uneasy feeling in you because she does this often enough so that you never know for sure where she is on her commitments for class assignments.

Question: Which feeling word would be most appropriate to add to your message?

_____ a. ". . . I feel angry . . ."

_____ b. ". . . I feel upset . . ."

_____ c. ". . . I'm feeling worried . . ."

Responses:

c. (Most Appropriate) Being worried carries with it the sense of concern, agitation and the unknown quality of the situation. It indicates a serious problem that causes you to think a lot about it. Probably it is more on target to say you feel worried than to say you're upset or irritated.

a. (Inappropriate) A general sense of anger conveys no special information about the particular situation here.

b. (Inappropriate) "Upset" could cover a range of behaviors from a type of stomachache to grief over the loss of a loved one. Using that word here adds nothing significant to your message.

Don't Use Stronger Feelings to Build Your Case

Again, the power of assertion lies in its simplicity. It is a statement of genuine concern about a problem behavior from one person to another. To convince another to change his or her behavior, you need to indicate a legitimate feeling about its effect on your life.

To say, "I am outraged that you are three minutes late for our meeting after we've discussed the importance of punctuality . . ." would make that situation laughable. It is better to use a word that expresses how you really feel, such as *annoyed.* This makes your whole message congruent and therefore more believable to the person whose behavior you want to change.

Please read the following situation and select the best response.

Situation: Kevin frequently comes into your apartment to borrow your records without asking. Although he usually returns them, it is his not asking that upsets you. You have spoken with him on two other occasions about the problem. You feel awkward about asking him whether he took a record which you have just discovered to be missing.

Question: Which feeling word should you use to assert to Kevin?

   _____ a. ". . . I'm feeling abused and manipulated . . ."

   _____ b. ". . . I'm feeling irritated . . ."

   _____ c. ". . . I am outraged by your behavior . . ."

Responses:

b. (Most Appropriate) This seems closest to describing the current situation for you. Not only are you being infringed by the record-borrowing, but now one is missing.

a. (Inappropriate) You don't need feeling words this strong to have a successful assertion. There may be a variety of reasons for your inability at this time to ask Kevin about the missing record. "Abused" and "manipulated" are unlikely to help you accomplish your goals.

c. (Inappropriate) "Outrage" would seem to be a strong word for most people in this situation. You spoke twice to Kevin about the problem. Your needs are not getting met and you want to confront Kevin to change the problem behavior. A different level of energy, perhaps something like "aggravated" or "discouraged", is probably closer to the real feeling at this point.

Don't Use "Victim" Words

The primary goal of assertion is to change another's problem behavior. Words such as *hurt, disappointed,* and *let down* are not focused on that purpose. These words have a tendency to result in people feeling guilty instead of enabling them to change their behavior. "I feel hurt," for example, seems directed toward letting the other person know that he or she did not meet your expectations. The behavior change you want then becomes secondary.

Please read the following situation and select the best response.

Situation: You are the principal of a school. One of your teachers, Justin Perman, has agreed to do better at confronting students in the class for their poor discipline. This agreement resulted from several meetings you had with Justin to solve the problem. This new behavior means a lot to you because parents of some of the children are taking up a lot of your time complaining about class discipline. Prior to this meeting you had spent time in the classroom working with problem students. You have also spent time coaching the teacher in assertion. Things had been improving, but yesterday you received four calls from upset parents. You felt your work was meaningless and the problem was right back where you started.

Question: Which feeling word is most appropriately directed to getting your needs met?

   _____ a. ". . . I'm feeling frustrated . . ."

   _____ b. ". . . I feel disappointed . . ."

   _____ c. ". . . I feel let down . . ."

Response:

a. (Most Appropriate) You are frustrated about the result you didn't get with this problem solving time and let Justin know your feelings. The message to Justin is: The result wasn't achieved!

b. (Inappropriate) By saying that you were "disappointed", you are focusing mostly on Justin's relationship with you, not the problem behavior. The emotion is centered around Justin not living up to your expectations. The message to Justin is: You let me down!

c. (Inappropriate) This message to Justin seems to be: You didn't do it for me! The implication is that pleasing you is a higher priority than changing a problem behavior to get better results.

Describing the Negative Effect on Your Life

The third component of the three-part assertion message is a description of the negative effect the problem behavior has on you. This is another piece of information you need to tell a person whose behavior is affecting your life in a negative way. Even when you describe the problem behavior itself accurately, if you don't communicate the problems that behavior is causing you in a way that helps the other person understand the negative impact the behavior has on your life, he or she is not as likely to change the problem behavior.

In developing the "negative effect" component of the three-part assertion message, the following guidelines are helpful:

1. Specify the effect as concretely as possible.
2. State the effect on *your* life.
3. Avoid using reasons.
4. Don't exaggerate the effect.
5. Don't use an effect that "sounds good" but isn't true.

Each of these guidelines is elaborated below. The multiple-choice exercises provided in the subsections covering the guidelines are followed by brief discussions of the most appropriate response and the inappropriate responses for each exercise.

Specify the Effect as Concretely as Possible

People are not easily persuaded to change their behavior. Their openness to change (other than in response to a threat of punishment) usually depends upon your ability to convince them that their behavior is somehow affecting your life in a negative way. The best way to do this is to state, as concretely as possible, what the effect is. Concrete and tangible effects usually involve your time, property, money, or health. Some ways to "measure" the effects on your life of someone else's behavior are in terms of what that behavior costs you, such as:

- Additional time spent ("I have to take longer to complete my work").
- Increased expenditures ("I can't keep within my budget").
- Damaged health ("I have an allergy and can hardly breathe").

Please read the following situation and select the best response.

Situation: You are a manager responsible for the output of a department. The nature of your work requires you to schedule each person's activities carefully, in advance, to coordinate with what the others are doing. Because of your need for advance planning, you establish a policy in your department requiring all employees to give you at least three or four days' notice when they want to take a vacation day. Most comply with the policy, but one person usually waits until the last minute to let you know. She did it again this morning on a day when you were counting on her to complete some calculations needed by two of your other workers. You determine to speak to her about this problem to resolve it so it doesn't happen again.

Question: Which phrase is "measurable" in a way most likely to convince this employee that your life is negatively affected by her behavior.

_____ a. ". . . because I can't get my work done."

_____ b. ". . . because I have to spend extra time reworking my schedule to keep output up when I could be doing other things."

_____ c. ". . . because we've spoken about this before and it shouldn't have happened again."

Responses:

b. (Most appropriate) You spent time making up a schedule. If you knew in advance that this person would not be at work, you could have taken that into account. Now, you must re-do the work you've done and the extra work was not necessary.

a. (Inappropriate) This might be true to some degree. However, this statement is too general and vague to convince the person that your life is genuinely affected.

c. (Inappropriate) This statement blames the other person more than it informs her. Your goal of changing her behavior will best be met by telling her how you are affected by what she does. Remember, you are trying to get a voluntary behavior change, rather than to use your position power.

State the Effect on Your Life

Unless you show the other person how your own life is directly affected by what he or she does, the other will probably not be motivated to change the behavior. Instead, the conversation will usually be diverted from your assertion to an argument about whether or not the effect really bothers you.

If the effect is on your life or work or the unit for which you are responsible, the other person will usually see that as an effect on you. Generally, you should avoid stating an effect on someone else. Examples of stating an effect on someone else are:

". . . because Beth has a more difficult time writing her reports."

". . . because you won't meet your deadlines."

". . . because it disturbs Tamara's sleep."

Please read the following situation and select the best response.

Situation: You work in a studio with two other artists. The three of you are responsible for keeping the place orderly. One of your group leaves her ceramic materials unwashed and the place in a general mess. You have asked her three times to help keep the studio orderly. When you got to work this morning, you again had to clean up the studio before you could start work. You have decided to confront her.

Question: Which statement shows the effect of this person's behavior on your life?

_____ a. ". . . because if you get away with it, the others will start doing it."

_____ b. ". . . because we will have to clean up."

_____ c. ". . . because I must do the clean up myself."

Responses:

c. (Most appropriate) You are concerned primarily with how the work is going to get done. Your statement indicates what you will have to do (the effect on your life) to clean up.

a. (Inappropriate) This effect is probably accurate. It does not, however, tell the person how that result affects you. If you are most worried about what the others will begin doing, to get to the measurable effect on your life, you should ask this question: "If other people start doing it, what price will I pay?" The answer will be that you will have to spend additional time to clean up.

b. (Inappropriate) The use of "we" instead of "I" indicates an effect of which I can't be certain. You can only account for the effect on you personally. If you use "we" you open yourself to a comment "Sally doesn't see it that way" and you are then involved in an argument.

Avoid Using Reasons

Explaining why you are upset about someone's behavior, rather than how it affects you, does not help persuade the other person to change the behavior. The other still might not see that his or her behavior makes any major, concrete difference in your life. For example, when another is repeatedly late for staff meetings, you might correctly assert: "When you are late for staff meetings, as with the meeting today, I feel annoyed, because I then need to take extra time to bring you up to date on material you missed." Using reasons for the negative effect decreases the effectiveness of the assertion message by obscuring the negative effect. Some reasons might be:

". . . because knowing this material is important for your job."

". . . because I can't be responsible for always keeping you up to date."

Please read the following situation and select the best response.

Situation: One of Susan's job responsibilities is to proofread and edit the chancellor's reports before they are passed out to the Executive Board members each month. Sometimes Susan forgets or runs out of time and she distributes the copies without being proofed. The last time this happened, one of the Board members mentioned to the Chancellor that he saw three or four errors, saying "it looked a little unprofessional." The Chancellor decides to speak to Susan again about this part of her work assignment.

Question: Which statement shows the effect of Susan's behavior on the Chancellor, rather than a reason for the Chancellor being upset?

_____ a. ". . . because I lose stature with the Board."

_____ b. ". . . because I am held responsible for it."

_____ c. ". . . because I don't have the report I want for the meeting."

Responses:

a. (Most appropriate) The effect on the Chancellor's life is that he is looked upon with less favor by the Board. This can have many serious future consequences for him if the problem behavior continues.

b. (Inappropriate) The reason the Chancellor is upset is because he will be held accountable. This does not tell Susan how the Chancellor's life will be affected by this accountability. In response to this reason, Susan might simply say, "Don't worry about it, they know you're doing a good job." She couldn't make this kind of response if the Chancellor had told her the effect on his life.

c. (Inappropriate) "Not having a report" is not the reason the Chancellor is upset. It is not a statement showing the effect on his life. The effect can be determined by asking "So what?" How am I affected because I don't have this report? The answer might be any number of things, and whichever one it is should become the "effect" statement.

Don't Exaggerate the Effect

People will accept the fact that you have a problem if you can legitimately demonstrate to them how your life is affected in a negative way. It is usually more truthful to say, for example, that as a result of the other's behavior, you will have "a more difficult time" doing something than to say you "can't" do it. Others are likely to believe that their behaviors cause you problems but are not likely to believe that they make your task or life impossible.

Please read the following situation and select the best response.

Situation: Your best friend, Jaret, with whom you have played raquetball for over two years, has not showed up for an agreed upon raquetball game for the third time this semester. You are very irritated with his behavior, since it is difficult to get a partner at the last minute. After you have built it into your schedule and are really counting on it, the late cancellation makes it almost impossible for you to play.

Question: Which effect on your life is Jaret more apt to believe?

_____ a. ". . . because I never get my exercise."

_____ b. ". . . because of your behavior, I can't play raquetball."

_____ c. ". . . because it is difficult to get a partner at the last minute and I often end up not playing."

80

Responses:

c. (Most appropriate) The effect on your life is an unnecessary and unfair increase in your time and energy.

b. (Inappropriate) You can play raquetball. You might have to practice yourself or you might not be happy about the partner you can get at the last moment. But you can play. An exaggeration here will lessen the impact of your legitimate concern.

a. (Inappropriate) "Never" is an absolute—doubtfully true. The other person will probably say something like this to you: "What do you mean never?" Another problem with this message is that not getting any exercise is probably an exaggeration. It might be true at this time, but not always.

Don't Use an Effect That "Sounds Good" but Isn't True

Many people are strongly tempted to ensure the success of their assertion by making it stronger than it actually is. Their belief is usually that "my negative effect probably isn't good enough."

Do not search for the "best" effect. The more you try to increase the stakes, the more you will decrease the effectiveness of your message. Instead, determine the real effect on your life and state it. Assertion generally works because of its simple honesty—one human being telling another, clearly and without a hidden agenda, about a specific behavior that is troublesome and how it affects his or her life. Most people respond to this sincere, straightforward approach.

Please read the following situation and select the best response.

Situation: Emily dislikes Gay's habit of coming to her to complain about others in the office. Emily decides to put together an assertion message to see if she can confront Gay about this behavior.

Question: Which is the real effect on Emily's life and the statement most likely to change Gay's behavior?

_____ a. ". . . because I don't have enough time to complete my work."

_____ b. ". . . because I don't like talking about other people."

_____ c. ". . . because it disrupts my flow of concentration and I lose good ideas."

Responses:

b. (Most appropriate) Emily doesn't like the content of Gay's conversation. Emily appropriately addresses herself to this issue.

a. (Inappropriate) Emily is more upset about the "gossipy" nature of Gay's conversation than with the fact that it intrudes on her work time. The effect that is real for her—the talking about others—should be the focus.

c. (Inappropriate) This disruption of "concentration flow" is probably not accurate. It sounds like a better reason to assert, but it is not the current negative effect on Emily's life. Gay probably won't "buy" it, and therefore, will probably not change her behavior.

Assembling Three-Part Assertion Messages

As mentioned earlier, assertion messages can be used either to defend or to express appreciation. In the following two sections, exercises are provided to help you become more skillful in formulating both types of three-part assertion messages.

Defending Assertion Messages

A three-part defending assertion message always contains a statement telling the other person what he or she did (a description of the problem behavior), your feelings about the problem, and how your life was negatively affected in a measurable way. It is normally used to defend personal rights, usually involving your time, property, money, or health. This type of assertion message is effective because there is a high probability that it will alter the other person's troublesome behavior without diminishing the other's self-esteem or damaging the relationship. The three-part defending assertion message does not judge or blame the other. It merely discloses the feelings you experienced in response to the other's behavior that has infringed on you in some way. The other person remains free to arrive at his or her solution to the intrusion that meets your needs.

The defending assertion message should be succinct and stated in one sentence. Although the three parts of the message may be given in any order, it is preferable to begin by learning the sequence presented earlier in the chapter. To review, the three-part sequence is:

"When you _____ I feel _____ because _____ ."

1. "When you _____ . . ." Concrete, specific, nonjudgmental description of the behavior that is infringing on your space. (Direct and short, not blaming.)

2. ". . . I feel _____ . . ." Appropriate, accurate disclosure of your feelings about the other's behavior.

3. ". . . because _____ ." Description of the concrete and tangible negative effects of the other's behavior on you. What it means or what it costs you. (Should be buyable, publicly observable and make sense to the other person.)

EXAMPLE:

Behavior Description	*Feelings*	*Effect*
When you don't show up for the staff meeting on time as we agreed, such as yesterday's conference	I feel aggravated	I need to take extra time bringing you up to date.

Read the following statements and write an appropriate three-part assertion message for each. Use the example as a guide.

1. You are the president of the student council. Your vice-president is continually absent from meetings, causing you to meet with him later to bring him up to date on material discussed.

When you _____

I feel _____

because _____

2. You work in an office with two other secretaries. The three of you are responsible for keeping the place orderly. One of your group leaves her coffee cups unwashed and the place in a general mess. You have asked her three times to help keep the office orderly. When you got to work this morning, you again had to clean up the office before you could start work.

When you _____

I feel _____

because _____

3. You are a teacher. You have reserved some audio-visual equipment to use today. Another teacher took the equipment you reserved for your use at the time you reserved it. There is no other equipment available for you to use and the audio-visual material was the key to your lesson plan today. This is the third time you have had the problem with this teacher.

When you _____

I feel _____

because _____

4. Sheldon, the bookstore cashier with whom you work, spends more time chatting with customers than serving them. The lines get longer and longer, and people are genuinely angry and irritated when they finally arrive at your register for service. As a co-worker, you are disturbed about Sheldon's behavior.

When you   _____

I feel   _____

because   _____

5. Aunt Marie is always bringing up her health problems at every family gathering often interrupting the conversation to do so. You find this personally irritating.

When you   _____

I feel   _____

because   _____

6. You ride to school with your neighbor. She is late for the fourth time in three weeks, causing you to be late for class.

When you   _____

I feel   _____

because   _____

7. The roving science teacher left the classroom in a mess for the fourth week in a row. You have had to rush to clean the room up for your own class the following period.

When you   _____

I feel   _____

because   _____

8. The personnel director always calls meetings to begin about half an hour before the end of the working day and the meetings run on and on. You want to be home on time to prepare the evening meal and you are late every time he holds one of these late meetings.

When you   _____

I feel   _____

because   _____

Appreciating Assertion Message

An appreciating assertion message is a two or three part message normally used to impact or influence another. This type of assertion message communicates the positive consequence of another's behavior on you and the feelings you experience in response to that behavior.

The appreciative assertion message should be succinct and stated in one sentence. Although the parts of the message may be given in any order, it is preferable to begin by learning the following sequence:

"When you _____ I feel _____ because _____ ."

1. "When you _____ . . ." Concrete, specific description of the other's behavior that positively affected you.
2. ". . . I feel _____ . . ." Appropriate, accurate disclosure of your feelings about the other's behavior.
3. ". . . because _____ ." Description of the concrete and tangible positive effects of the other's behavior on you (if appropriate).

Example:

Behavior Description:	*Feeling:*	*Effect:*
When you make the orange juice in the morning,	I feel cared for,	because I'm rushed in the morning and wouldn't take the time myself.

Read the following statements and write an appropriate appreciative assertion message of two or three parts for each one. Use the example as a guide.

1. Your husband rushed home from his job to prepare a meal and cake to celebrate your father's birthday, since he knew you were going to be detained at a late meeting and would be unable to make the preparations yourself.

   When you _____

   I feel _____

   because _____

2. You are the Principal of a large high school. All faculty members have made a special effort to attend every meeting since the initiation of the North Central Study for Accreditation.

   When you _____

   I feel _____

   because _____

3. The director of the library where you work always invites you to library functions. You feel especially pleased and honored to be included in important gatherings.

   When you _____

   I feel _____

   because _____

4. A resource person gave a special workshop to the dorm residents on self-defense. You thought the material was very relevant and the situational examples right on target.

   When you _____

   I feel _____

   because _____

5. The president of the company where you work uses a participative, shared responsibility model in the administration of the company. This effort has resulted in a high degree of involvement in company activity.

   When you _____

   I feel _____

   because _____

6. The social worker has the ability to really hear special needs of the clients and respond to them in concrete ways.

   When you _____

   I feel _____

   because _____

7. The facilitator of the workshop is doing an outstanding job. You are especially pleased with the low-key presentation.

When you   _____

I feel   _____

because   _____

Assertion Messages: Personal Examples

The Assertion Messages: Personal Examples Worksheet is designed to help you identify assertion situations in your own personal or professional life and formulate appropriate assertion messages that will communicate to the other person his or her infringement or positive behavior, your feelings about that behavior, and (if appropriate) the effect that behavior has on your life.

Please complete the worksheet, providing (if possible) at least three personal examples. The following guidelines will help you complete the worksheet columns:

1. Times at which you felt infringed upon or pleased—general area of infringement or positive behavior by a particular person.

    Defending assertion example: Unwashed dishes from snacks left in the office coffee room.

    Appreciating assertion example: Finding the office-supplies cabinet well stocked.

2. *Specific instance*—one particular occasion of infringement or positive behavior that occurred recently.

    Defending assertion example: Coffee cups—complete with ants!—that I found this morning in the office coffee room.

    Appreciating assertion example: This afternoon, when I was looking for a box of staples.

3. *Description of role*—your role in the situation, such as: son, daughter, brother, sister, associate, colleague, student.

    Defending assertion example: Associate.

    Appreciating assertion example: Supervisor.

4. *Name of individual*—specific person you relate to in that role.

    Defending assertion example: Kathleen.

    Appreciating assertion example: Marilyn (my secretary).

5. *Assertion, or "I," message*—an assertion message to deliver to the person regarding the specific area of infringement or positive behavior.

    Defending assertion example: "When you leave your dirty dishes in the office coffee room—such as the coffee cups on the table this morning—I feel irritated, because it makes more work for me."

    Appreciating assertion example: "When you keep the office supplies cabinet well stocked, I feel grateful, because I don't have to waste time running all over the building whenever I need something."

Assertion Messages: Personal Examples Worksheet

"When you _____ , I feel _____ , because _____ ."

Brief description of instance you felt infringed upon or pleased.	First draft message.	Revision.	Final message.

Message Sending

After a defending assertion message has been thought out and carefully worded, it is important to rehearse the message and then arrange an appropriate time and place to deliver it to the other who is infringing on you.

The sequence shown below is followed when delivering the defending assertion message:

1. *Send the assertion, or "I," message* ("When you _____ I feel _____ because _____ ").
2. *Silence* (wait for a response or a solution).
3. *Reflective listen to the other's response.*
4. *Recycle the above three steps.*
5. *Express appreciation for the solution.*

Emotional Energy

When sending an assertion message, it is important for you to remember to reflective listen to the other's response, since that will help reduce defensiveness and lower his or her high energy level. Likewise, it is important for you to remember to resend the assertion message after reflective listening, since the message will have a greater effect now that the other's "emotional energy" has been lowered by the reflective listening (that is, the other will hear the message more completely). Figure 24 illustrates the use of assertion and reflective listening skills to lower the other's "emotional energy" during the assertion process. You will be able to pinpoint the exact timing to re-assert by getting a "yes" response from the other, as indicated in figure 24.

Altering the Three-Part Assertion Process

The circumstances under which you alter the assertion process are:

- You provide additional information after which you return to the assertion process.
- The other offers you an acceptable solution after which you express appreciation.
- You receive new information from the other. In this case, you may:
  —modify your own position.
  —problem solve.
- The other brings up an irrelevant topic. In this case, you would listen to the content and then return to the original focus.
- The other persists in treating you inhumanely. In this case, you will alter the message or end the conversation.
- You move to problem solving when the other refuses to modify his or her behavior.

Assertion Difficulties

Some common difficulties in using three-part assertion messages are:

- *Undershooting or overshooting*—reporting a mild feeling of "upset" when "furious" actually fits the situation or reporting a strong feeling when a mild one would be more appropriate.
- *Sender too much in grips of anger*—the level of anger is too high to reflective listen effectively.
- *Hit and run*—sending a single message and stopping.
- *Forgetting to reflective listen*—not remembering to reflective listen to the other's defensive response.

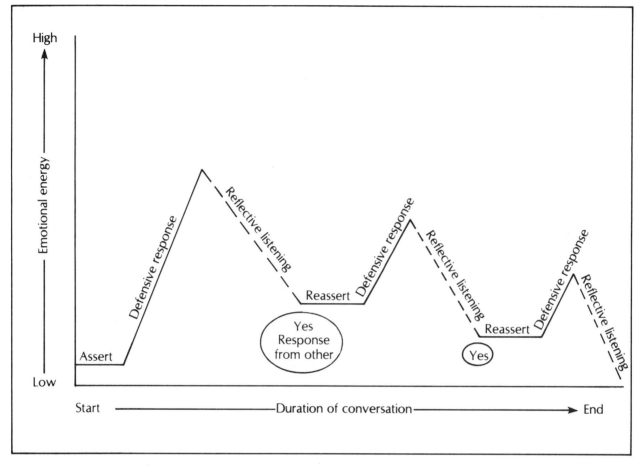

Figure 24. Lowering emotional energy through assertion and reflective listening.

- *Forgetting to reassert after reflective listening*—not remembering to send the message a second and third time.
- *Repetition*—sending exactly the same message over again after the second assertion.
- *Not asserting directly to the source*—sending the message to a friend when another is the infringing party.

Guidelines for Skill Practice

The skill practice sessions for assertion will take place in small groups of three or four, consisting of a sender, a receiver, and one or two observers. (Such a practice session was illustrated in Chapter 1, figure 1.) The roles of the sender, receiver, and observer(s) in assertion skill practice are as follows:

Sender:
1. Describes the situation to the other so that the other will be able to respond.
2. Sends assertion message, using appropriate assertion and reflective listening skills.

Receiver: Responds defensively (offers two defensive responses), without using any skills.

Observer(s):
1. Observes the process.
2. Keeps track of time.
3. Leads the feedback and evaluation by:
   a. inviting the receiver to express how well he or she felt asserted to.
   b. inviting the sender to express reactions to the use of skills.
   c. making observations and positive suggestions.

During the feedback session following the skill practice, members of the small group should concentrate on the following:

1. Focus on the feelings first.
2. Share progress made.
3. Share one area you need to work on.
4. Share learnings and concerns.

Physical Components of Assertion

In assertion it is essential that your body language be congruent with your verbal messages. With both your words and physical components, you are wanting to communicate that the issue is important to you and that you want both yourself and the other party to attempt to deal with the issue now.

Listed below are a number of factors that contribute to the overall effectiveness of an assertion. In sending an assertion message, you should consider these carefully to be sure they support your intended message.

- *Eye contact*—Direct, concentrated eye contact that communicates: "This is important to me."
- *Posture*—Lean slightly toward the other, with a posture that communicates the seriousness of the message.
- *Gestures*—Should support the force of the communication.
- *Facial expression*—Needs to be congruent with the message.
- *Voice*—Appropriate tone, rate, volume, and inflection should be used.
- *Timing and location*—Select to ensure privacy and freedom from interruption.
- *Content of message*—Two- or three-part "I message" rather than "you message." Reflective listen to responses.

Handling Difficult Assertion Defenses

In some situations, the other responds to an assertion message in a nonverbal way, offering no words to which to reflective listen. In each of these cases, you need to reflective listen not to the words but to what you observe in the other's behavior—e.g., silence, leaving, disgust, crying, or laughter.

- *When the other is silent:*
    —"I can see you're really overcome by what I've said."
    —"You're so jarred right now you can't think of anything to say."
    —"I've sort of wiped you out right now."
- *When the other leaves:*
    —"You're so upset by this that you're walking out."
    —"You really want to get away from me right now."
    —"You're so concerned about what I've said that you're leaving."
- *When the other looks disgusted:*
    —"It seems to you as if I'm making a big thing out of nothing."
    —"I really seem thin-skinned to you."
    —"It's as if I'm making a mountain out of a molehill."
    —"You think I've got a lot of nerve bringing this up when I've got my faults, too."

- *When the other cries:*
    —"This is really upsetting for you."

    —"You're feeling extremely hurt by this."

    —"I've really embarrassed you."

    —"My message brought a lot of pain for you."
- *When the other laughs:*
    —"This all seems pretty silly to you."

    —"I appear pretty funny to you."

    —"You seem to find my concerns quite amusing."

Skilled Alternatives to High-Risk Responses

As noted in Chapter 3, a "high-risk response" is a response in a listening situation that tends to raise the level of defensiveness in the other or to take the focus off the other. Usually, the use of high-risk responses represents an attempt to achieve a worthwhile purpose. However, you can normally achieve your purpose more effectively by employing an alternative, skilled response. Shown below are some high-risk responses, followed by suggested alternative skilled responses:

HIGH-RISK RESPONSE	PURPOSE	SKILLED APPROACH
Ordering	Ordering is an attempt to get your personal goals met.	Normally, sending an assertion message is the most effective way of getting your personal goals met.
Threatening	Threatening is normally an attempt to get your personal goals met.	Sending an assertion message is usually the most effective way of getting your personal goals met.
Moralizing	Moralizing is an attempt to help the other behave in ways that are good, fitting, true, appropriate, etc.	Reflective listening will help the other develop an internal system of evaluation that will benefit him or her in both the present and subsequent situations.
Advising	Advising is suggesting how the other person might get his or her personal goals met in the most effective way.	Since the other has better information about his or her personal goals, reflective listening is a means of helping the other find the solution that is most appropriate and acceptable. Sometimes, after a long period of reflective listening, you can introduce the problem-solving process should the other person appear struck, or blocked.
Logical arguments	Offering logical arguments is an approach intended to help another see an issue clearly and decide wisely.	Reflective listening allows the other person to explore his or her problem, need, or opportunity more objectively and clearly. The acceptance that is communicated through reflective

HIGH-RISK RESPONSE	PURPOSE	SKILLED APPROACH
		listening enhances the other's ability to solve his or her own problem. In addition, you can help the other by facilitating the problem-solving process, if this seems appropriate.
Questioning	Questioning attempts to get the other person to say more or leads into your giving advice to the other.	When the purpose of questioning is to facilitate the other person's talking, reflective listening will accomplish this more effectively. Likewise, when the purpose of questioning is to advise or is a preface to giving advice, reflective listening skills are more appropriate.
Judging	Judging another often occurs when your personal goals are not getting met. The judgment may be made about an area unrelated to your unmet goals.	Assertion messages enable you to get your personal goals met more effectively, in ways that are much more accepting of the other person and less judgmental.
Praising	Praising is often intended to let another know how delighted you are about something the other has achieved.	An appreciating assertion message lets the other person know specifically what about his or her behavior is appreciated. Sometimes, the message describes the concrete and tangible effect the other's behavior has on your life, which helps the other receive and accept the message more readily.
Diagnosing	Diagnosing or interpreting is normally an attempt to help the other person see his or her situation more clearly.	When you diagnose another person, the other often experiences this as threatening. Reflective listening enables the other to act upon new understanding based on self-diagnosis. Normally, self-diagnosis is an essential step in behavior change.
Name-calling	Name-calling is normally intended to discharge anger and get your personal goals met.	Assertion messages are a more effective means of getting your personal goals met while "owning" any strong feelings involved.
Reassuring	Reassurance, when it's not manipulative or an attempt to avoid experiencing the other's discomfort, is usually offered to comfort and/or strengthen the other person.	Reflective listening can assist another to experience difficult circumstances in life and face them with courage. Interested silence is especially helpful in serious problems or grief situations.
Diverting	Diverting is an attempt to move the other person to a more comfortable, safe subject.	In such circumstances, it is more appropriate to send an assertion message letting the other person know you are not able to deal with the matter or with him or her at this time.

Conflict Management

Conflict is an all-pervasive element in our society. Although conflicts may end up in destruction and even death, conflicts may also result in increased effectiveness, enhanced relationships, and further goal attainment. Indeed, in human terms conflict is one of the "engines of evolution" that allows us to learn, progress, and grow. Therefore, our goal as skilled communicators is not to attempt to do away with conflict but to skillfully manage conflict to further its constructive capabilities.

In this chapter, we will explore definitions and views of conflict, conflict-management styles, and the advantages and disadvantages of various approaches to the handling of disputes and differences. Also included are specific strategies and exercises to enhance your effectiveness in dealing with conflicts of needs and conflicts of values—strategies that allow you to get goals met without damaging relationships.

Conflict

Conflict is an expressed struggle in which two or more interdependent parties are experiencing strong emotion resulting from a perceived difference in needs or values.

Conflict is typified by a discord of thought, feeling, or action occurring between people, groups, organizations, communities, or nations that must interact with each other. Conflict involves differences that are important enough to distance or alienate the involved parties if left unresolved. To handle conflict effectively, both the emotional and substantive consequences arising from such differences must be taken into account.

A conflict situation exists when:

1. At least two parties are involved.
2. Mutually exclusive needs or mutually exclusive values either exist or are perceived to exist.
3. Interaction is characterized by strong emotion and behavior designed to defeat, reduce, or suppress the opponent.
4. The parties face each other with mutually opposing actions as they attempt to gain a forward position of power relative to the other.

Conflict management is the process of becoming aware of a conflict, diagnosing its nature, and employing an appropriate methodology to diffuse the emotional energy involved and enable the disputing parties to understand and resolve their differences.

Although conflict can emerge both within and between groups as well as between individuals, this book focuses on inter-personal conflict.

Ambivalence Toward Conflict

If you were to freely associate the word *conflict,* three kinds of responses would likely emerge:

1. One set of terms would have grisly and *negative* connotations: war, death, destruction, discord, disorder, aggression, rape, violence.

2. A second set of terms would have *positive* connotations: adventure, opportunity, drama, fun, excitement, development.

3. A third set of terms would be relatively *neutral:* tension, competition, scarcity, mediation, bargaining.

Some of us would respond with terms from two sets or even from all three. Such results generally indicate a basic ambivalence toward conflict.

The ambivalence we feel toward conflict stems partly from deeply ingrained values promoted by society, partly from the nature of conflict itself, and partly from the tendency to discount the important role of emotions in interpersonal dealings. We will examine each of these factors briefly.

Social Barriers to Conflict Management

Although in the context of this learning experience conflict is viewed as an opportunity for growth, this goal in itself is in conflict with several dominant values in our society. Children are typically trained to avoid confrontation in areas of deep-seated values. They are taught not to question positions based on beliefs—political or religious, for example. Many people seem to value an aggressive openness on insignificant matters while at the same time maintaining a smooth social facade on significant ones. To many, assertive problem solving based on an open acceptance of conflict is actually bad manners.

Interdependence

Conflict occurs within a context of interdependence. An extreme example is a poker game, where the gains of one party are directly related to the losses of the other. If the parties in conflict were not interdependent—that is, if the actions of one party did not have some consequence for the other party and vice-versa—it is unlikely that conflict would occur. This helps explain the fear of conflict. At best, conflict disrupts the order and established functioning of the group or interpersonal relationship in which it occurs, and at worst, it leads to the destruction of the group or relationship. However, if interdependence has value for everyone in the system and everyone perceives this, then the interdependence can offer hope for constructive resolution. In this situation, the interdependence is a force toward creating some mutually acceptable solution for the conflict and usually results in the improvement of the health of the group or relationship.

Emotions in Conflict Situations

Emotions play a major role in interpersonal behavior. No matter how prescribed role requirements may be, an individual will react to situations and problems in a way that is based on his or her experience and training. The reaction always includes an emotional component. When people appear to be moved only by ideas and to be concerned only for correctness, this probably indicates they have lost touch with this emotional component. They may, in short, have ceased to recognize their feelings but are still influenced by them.

This viewpoint sometimes causes work groups to ignore feelings, to insist on a "strictly business" approach to problems. In these situations, feelings are forced to operate "under the table," creating hidden agendas.

Deep emotional commitments often create tension that allows conflict to build on irrational factors. Hostility generated in a superior-subordinate disagreement, for instance, at times gets redirected onto less-powerful subordinates or outsiders, perhaps those in different functional groups. Information becomes distorted to support a particular stand, with personal hostility often sanctioned.

The consequence of suppressing or ignoring emotions is often conflict and unrealistic decision making. The test of a good decision—one that will be carried out wholeheartedly—is not whether it has been made unemotionally, but whether all of the emotions involved have been expressed, heard, recognized, and taken into account.

Positive Results of Conflict

Conflict can bring opportunity, drama, development, and growth to individuals, groups, and organizations. Conflict can often increase group cohesion and trust and lead to more effective organizational performance. Conflict in group settings, when properly managed, can lead to increased motivation and productivity as well as to better personal adjustment of group members. Conflict can have integrating effects on ties between parties. It can stimulate the search for new facts and solutions, increase the conflicting parties' energy to perform the tasks required by the organization, and defuse more serious conflict.

Conflict need not be destructive or debilitating; it can often be approached in such a way as to be growth-producing and beneficial. This learning experience will focus on enhancing your understanding of conflict and will present specific skills for its effective management in interpersonal settings.

A Two-Dimensional Model of Conflict

Although you may not often think of it this way, everyone has his or her own characteristic approach, or style, when it comes to managing conflict. There are people who shrink away at the first signs of conflict, while others typically confront the conflict and seek a solution in which the goals of both parties will be met. There are people so concerned about the possibility of damaging their relationship with the other party that they concede their goals practically at the first sign of a conflict; while others attempt the "half a loaf" tactic, trying to achieve as much of their goal as possible while doing as little damage to the relationship as possible; while still others are so concerned with achieving their goal that they damage or destroy the relationship with the other party.

A person's conflict style is in fact determined by the amount of concern he or she has for the relationships and for the personal goals of the parties involved, as shown in the two-dimensional model of conflict (figure 25). The conflict styles, or approaches, represented by the differing degrees of emphasis that may be placed on the relationship between the conflicting parties and on their personal goals can briefly be described as follows:

1. *Collaborator.* The collaborator's approach to conflict is to manage it by maintaining interpersonal relationships and ensuring that both parties to the conflict achieve their personal goals. This attitude toward conflict is one in which the collaborator acts not only on behalf of his or her self-interest but on behalf of the opposing party's interests as well. Upon recognizing that a conflict exists, the collaborator utilizes appropriate conflict management methods to manage the conflict. This is a *win/win* posture, in which both the collaborator's stance toward conflict management and that of the other party are *win.*

2. *Compromiser.* The compromiser's approach to conflict is to assume that a win/win solution is not possible and adopt a negotiating stance that involves a little bit of winning and a little bit of losing with respect to both the goals and the relationships of the involved parties, with persuasion and manipulation dominating the style. The objective is to find some expedient, mutually acceptable solution which partially satisfies the parties involved. This is a *compromise* posture, with both the compromiser's stance toward conflict management and that of the other party being *mini-win/mini-lose.*

3. *Accommodator.* The accommodator's approach to conflict involves maintaining the interpersonal relationship at all cost, with little or no concern for the personal goals of the parties involved. Giving in, appeasing, and avoiding conflict are viewed as ways of protecting the relationship. This is a *yield-lose/win* posture, in which the accommodator's stance toward conflict management is to *yield-lose,* allowing the other to *win.*

4. *Controller.* The controller's approach to conflict is to take the necessary steps to ensure that his or her personal goals are met, whatever the cost to the relationship involved. Conflict is viewed as a win or lose proposition, with winning somehow equated with status and competence. This is a power oriented mode in which you use whatever power seems appropriate to win your own position, defend a position which you believe is correct, or simply attempt to win.

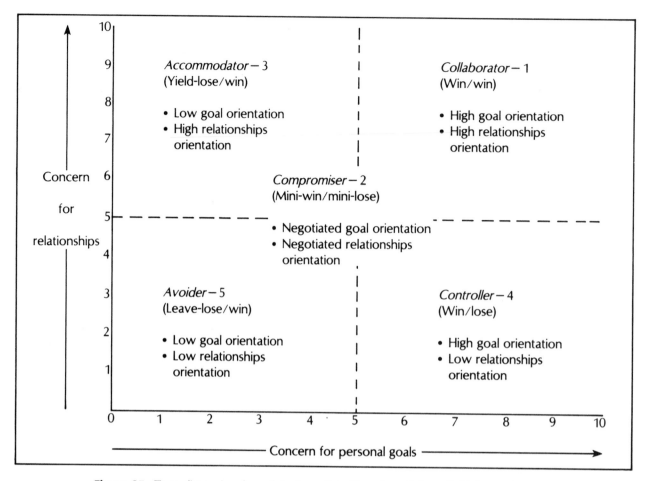

Figure 25. Two-dimensional model of conflict. (Based on Robert R. Blake and Jane S. Mouton, *Corporate Excellence Through GRID Organization Development* [Houston, Texas: Gulf Publishing Company, 1971], p. 11.)

5. *Avoider.* The avoider's approach to conflict is to view it as something to be shunned at all costs. A central theme of this style is hopelessness, which results in a high degree of frustration for all parties involved. Personal goals are usually not met, nor is the interpersonal relationship maintained in this style of conflict. It might take the form of diplomatically diverting an issue, postponing an issue until a better time, or simply withdrawing from a threatening situation. This is a leave-lose/win posture, in which the avoider's stance toward conflict management is to leave-lose, allowing the other to win.*

Three basic points to remember about people's styles/approaches to conflict are that:

1. People develop their styles/approaches for reasons that make sense to them.
2. No one style/approach is better than another in every situation.
3. People change their styles/approaches in order to adapt to the demands of new situations.

In the following section, you will be taking a look at the conflict style, or approach, that you presently use. In so doing, you will gain insight into not only your own conflict behavior but the conflict behavior of others who employ a style that is different from yours.

---

*For additional information on conflict styles, see Joyce H. Wilmot and William W. Wilmot, *Interpersonal Conflict* (New York: William C. Brown Company, 1978), pp. 23–46.

Conflict-Management Style

In this section you will have the opportunity to examine your own conflict-management style and techniques you tend to use in conflict situations, particularly under stress. The exercises that follow will enable you to gain insight into strategies you might choose to incorporate into your behavior in handling disputes and differences.

Conflict-Management Style Survey*

This Conflict-Management Style Survey has been designed to help you become more aware of your characteristic approach, or style, in managing conflict. In completing this survey, you are invited to respond by making choices that correspond with your typical behavior or attitudes in conflict situations.

Section 1: Survey

This survey identifies twelve situations that you are likely to encounter in your personal and professional lives. Please study each situation and the five possible behavioral responses or attitudes carefully and then allocate ten points between them to indicate your typical behavior, with the highest number of points indicating your strongest choice. Any response can be answered with from zero to ten points, as long as all five responses for a given situation add up to ten points, as shown in the following example:

EXAMPLE SITUATION: In responding to a request from another for help with a problem, you would:

0	A.	Clearly instruct him or her how to proceed.
2	B.	Enjoy the strategizing and the challenge.
7	C.	Help him or her take responsibility for the problem.
1	D.	Find it unnerving but agree to help.
0	E.	Avoid the invitation at all costs.
10		TOTAL

Please choose a single frame of reference (e.g., work-related conflicts, family conflicts, social conflicts) and keep that frame of reference in mind when responding to all the situations. And remember, as you complete this survey, that it is not a test. There are no right or wrong responses. The survey will be helpful to you only to the extent that your responses accurately represent your characteristic behavior or attitudes.

SITUATION 1: Upon experiencing strong feelings in a conflict situation, you would:

	A.	Enjoy the emotional release and sense of exhilaration and accomplishment.
	B.	Enjoy the strategizing involved and the challenge of the conflict.
3	C.	Become serious about how others are feeling and thinking.
1	D.	Find it frightening because you do not accept that differences can be discussed without someone's getting hurt.
0	E.	Become convinced that there is nothing you can do to resolve the issue.
10		TOTAL

*Based on Jay Hall's *Conflict Management Survey: A Survey of One's Characteristic Reaction to and Handling of Conflict Between Himself and Others* (The Woodlands, Texas: Telemetrics International, 1969).

SITUATION 2: Consider the following statements and rate them in terms of how characteristic they are of your personal beliefs:

_____ 0 _____ A. Life is conquered by those who believe in winning.

_____ 0 _____ B. Winning is rarely possible in conflict.

_____ 3 _____ C. No one has the final answer to anything, but each has a piece to contribute.

_____ 1 _____ D. In the last analysis, it is wise to turn the other cheek.

_____ 6 _____ E. It is useless to attempt to change a person who seems locked into an opposing view.

___10___ TOTAL

SITUATION 3: What is the best result that you expect from conflict?

_____ 4 _____ A. Conflict helps people face the fact that one answer is better than others.

_____ 1 _____ B. Conflict results in canceling out extremes of thinking so that a strong middle ground can be reached.

4 _____ 3 _____ C. Conflict clears the air and enhances commitment and results.

_____ 1 _____ D. Conflict demonstrates the absurdity of self-centeredness and draws people closer together in their commitment to each other.

_____ 0 _____ E. Conflict lessens complacency and assigns blame where it belongs.

___10___ TOTAL

SITUATION 4: When you are the person with the greater authority in a conflict situation, you would:

_____ 8 _____ A. Put it straight, letting the other know your view.

_____ 0 _____ B. Try to negotiate the best settlement you can get.

_____ 1 _____ C. Ask to hear the other's feelings and suggest that a position be found that both might be willing to try.

_____ 0 _____ D. Go along with the other, providing support where you can.

_____ 1 _____ E. Keep the encounter impersonal, citing rules if they apply.

___10___ TOTAL

SITUATION 5: When someone you care for takes an unreasonable position, you would:

4 5 6 7 _____ A. Lay it on the line, telling him or her that you don't like it.

_____ 2 _____ B. Let him or her know in casual, subtle ways that you are not pleased; possibly distract with humor; and avoid a direct confrontation.

3 4 _____ C. Call attention to the conflict and explore a mutually acceptable solution.

_____ 0 _____ D. Try to keep your misgivings to yourself.

_____ 1 _____ E. Let your actions speak for you by indicating depression or lack of interest.

___10___ TOTAL

SITUATION 6: When you become angry at a friend or colleague, you would:

_____ 1 _____ A. Just explode without giving it much thought.

_____ 0 _____ B. Try to smooth things over with a good story.

_____ 6 _____ C. Express your anger and invite him or her to respond.

_____ 0 _____ D. Try to compensate for your anger by acting the opposite of what you are feeling.

_____ 3 _____ E. Remove yourself from the situation.

___10___ TOTAL

SITUATION 7: When you find yourself disagreeing with other members of a group on an important issue, you would:

_8_ A. Stand by your convictions and defend your position.

_1_ B. Appeal to the logic of the group in the hope of convincing at least a majority that you are right.

_1_ C. Explore points of agreement and disagreement and the feelings of the group's members, and then search for alternatives that take everyone's views into account.

_0_ D. Go along with the rest of the group.

_0_ E. Not participate in the discussion and not feel bound by any decision reached.

_10_ TOTAL

SITUATION 8: When a single group member takes a position in opposition to the rest of the group, you would:

_0_ A. Point out publicly that the dissenting member is blocking the group and suggest that the group move on without him or her if necessary.

_3_ B. Make sure the dissenting member has a chance to communicate his or her objections so that a compromise can be reached.

_6_ C. Try to uncover why the dissenting member views the issue differently, so that the group's members can reevaluate their own positions.

_0_ D. Encourage the group's members to set the conflict aside and go on to more agreeable items on the agenda.

_1_ E. Remain silent, because it is best to avoid becoming involved.

_10_ TOTAL

SITUATION 9: When you see conflict emerging in a group, you would:

_0_ A. Push for a quick decision to ensure that the task is completed.

_0_ B. Avoid outright confrontation by moving the discussion toward a middle ground.

_4 5_ C. Share with the group your impression of what is going on, so that the nature of the impending conflict can be discussed.

_3_ D. Forestall or divert the conflict before it emerges by relieving the tension with humor.

_3_ E. Stay out of the conflict as long as it is of no concern to you.

_10_ TOTAL

SITUATION 10: In handling conflict between your group and another, you would:

_3_ A. Anticipate areas of resistance and prepare responses to objections prior to open conflict.

_0_ B. Encourage your group's members to be prepared by identifying in advance areas of possible compromise.

_6_ C. Recognize that conflict is healthy and press for the identification of shared concerns and/or goals.

_0_ D. Promote harmony on the grounds that the only real result of conflict is the destruction of friendly relations.

_1_ E. Have your group submit the issue to an impartial arbitrator.

_10_ TOTAL

SITUATION 11: In selecting a member of your group to represent you in negotiating with another group, you would choose a person who:

    0   A. Knows the rationale of your group's position and would press vigorously for your group's point of view.

    0   B. Would see that most of your group's judgments were incorporated into the final negotiated decision without alienating too many members of either group.

3 2   C. Would best represent the ideas of your group, evaluate these in view of judgments of the other group, and then emphasize problem-solving approaches to the conflict.

4 5   D. Is most skillful in interpersonal relations and would be openly cooperative and tentative in his or her approach.

    3   E. Would present your group's case accurately, while not making commitments that might result in obligating your group to a significantly changed position.

  10 TOTAL

SITUATION 12: In your view, what might be the reason for the failure of one group to collaborate with another?

    0   A. Lack of a clearly stated position, or failure to back up the group's position.

    5   B. Tendency of groups to force their leadership or representatives to abide by the group's decision, as opposed to promoting flexibility, which would facilitate compromise.

    5   C. Tendency of groups to enter negotiations with a win/lose perspective.

    0   D. Lack of motivation on the part of the group's membership to live peacefully with the other group.

    0   E. Irresponsible behavior on the part of the group's leadership, resulting in the leaders' placing emphasis on maintaining their own power positions rather than addressing the issues involved.

  10 TOTAL

Section 2: Scoring

Step 1

When you have completed all items in Section 1, write the number of points you assigned for each of the five responses for the twelve situations in the appropriate columns on the scoring form (figure 26). Add the total number of points for each column, then check that the totals for each column add up to 120.

Step 2

Transfer your column total scores onto the form showing the ideal order (figure 27).

Step 3

Transfer the style names, in order of the highest score first, onto figure 28, which shows your order, and then enter the scores in the adjacent blank spaces.

Step 4

Record your scores in the appropriate blanks on the Conflict-Management Styles Scoring Graph (figure 29). (You may wish to refresh your memory by reviewing the material describing the five conflict styles presented earlier in the subsection entitled A Two-Dimensional Model of Conflict.)

Situation	Response A	Response B	Response C	Response D	Response E	Total
1	4	2	3	1	0	10
2	0	0	3	1	6	10
3	4	1	4	1	0	10
4	8	0	1	0	1	10
5	~~6~~ 4	2	3 ~~4~~	0	1	10
6	1	0	6	0	3	10
7	8	1	1	0	0	10
8	0	3	6	0	1	10
9	0	0	4	3	3	10
10	3	0	6	0	1	10
11	0	0	3	4	3	10
12	0	5	5	0	0	10
TOTAL:	32 +	14 +	45 +	10 +	19 =	120

Figure 26. Scoring form.

	Style		Score
1.	Collaborator	(Column C)	45
2.	Compromiser	(Column B)	14
3.	Accommodator	(Column D)	10
4.	Controller	(Column A)	32
5.	Avoider	(Column E)	19
TOTAL:			120

Figure 27. Ideal order.

Choice	Style	Score
1st	Collaborator	45
2nd	Controller	32
3rd	Avoider	19
4th	Compromiser	14
5th	Accommodator	10
TOTAL:		120

Figure 28. Your order.

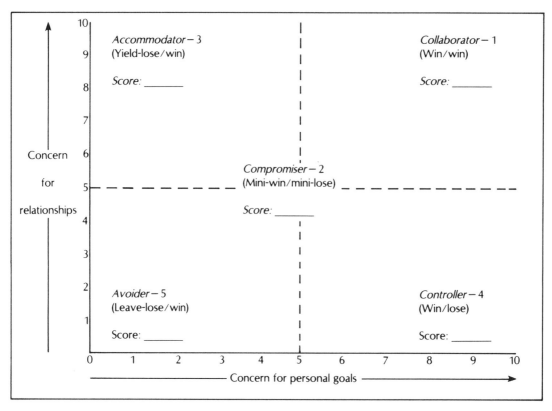

Figure 29. Conflict-management styles scoring graph. (Based on Robert R. Blake and Jane S. Mouton, *Corporate Excellence Through GRID Organization Development* [Houston, Texas: Gulf Publishing Company, 1971], p. 11.)

Conflict-Management Exercise*

The following is a list of thirty techniques that we typically use when we find ourselves in conflict with another:

1. Avoid the person.
2. Change the subject.
3. Try to understand the other person's point of view.
4. Try to turn the conflict into a joke.
5. Listen to the other's feelings.
6. Admit that you are wrong, even if you do not believe you are.
7. Give in.
8. Demand more than you would actually settle for.
9. Use your perceived superior power to prevent the other party from reaching his or her goal.
10. Try to find out specifically what you agree and disagree on to narrow down the conflict.
11. Try to reach a compromise.
12. Pretend to agree.
13. Move toward problem solving as best you can.
14. Get another person to decide who is right.
15. Suggest a way in which both you and the other person would gain something.

*Exercise adapted from Barbara Stanford, *Peacemaking: A Guide to Conflict Resolution for Individuals, Groups and Nations* (New York: Bantam, 1975), pp. 22–24; by permission of author.

16. Threaten the other person.
17. Fight it out physically.
18. Try to clarify what the other's goals are.
19. Whine or complain until you get your way.
20. Play the martyr: give in, but let the other person know how much you are suffering.
21. Apologize.
22. Give up some points in exchange for others.
23. Get the best deal you can no matter what.
24. Postpone it.
25. Go for a middle ground.
26. Avoid hurting the others feelings.
27. Get everything out in the open.
28. Sacrifice your interests for the relationship.
29. Split the difference.
30. Avoid controversy.

How Do You Handle Conflicts?	A = Frequently B = Occasionally C = Rarely		
Technique	A	B	C
1. Avoid the person.	X		
2. Change the subject.		X	
3. Try to understand the other person's point of view.		X	
4. Try to turn the conflict into a joke.			X
5. Listen to the other's feelings.	X		
6. Admit that you are wrong, even if you do not believe you are.			X
7. Give in.			X
8. Demand more than you would actually settle for.			X
9. Use your perceived superior power to prevent the other party from reaching his or her goal.		X	
10. Try to find out specifically what you agree and disagree on to narrow down the conflict.		X	
11. Try to reach a compromise.		X	
12. Pretend to agree.			X
13. Move toward problem solving as best you can.		X	
14. Get another person to decide who is right.		X	
15. Suggest a way in which both you and the other person would gain something.		X	
16. Threaten the other person.			X
17. Fight it out physically.			X
18. Try to clarify what the other's goals are.	X		
19. Whine or complain until you get your way.		X	
20. Play the martyr: give in, but let the other person know how much you are suffering.			X
21. Apologize.			X
22. Give up some points in exchange for others.		X	
23. Get the best deal you can no matter what.			X
24. Postpone it.			X
25. Go for a middle ground.		X	
26. Avoid hurting the others' feelings.		X	
27. Get everything out in the open.	X		
28. Sacrifice your interests for the relationship.			X
29. Split the difference.		X	
30. Avoid controversy.	X		

Figure 30. How do you handle conflicts?

Step 1

After each of the techniques in figure 30, indicate whether you use it frequently, occasionally or rarely.

Conflict Management Exercise Worksheet

Group or persons	Techniques you frequently use	Techniques you might use
Parents		
Children		
Brothers and sisters		
Spouse or other intimates		
Friends		
Peers		
People you do not know well		
Members of other racial groups		
Protesters		
Irritating complainants		
People in authority position over you		
Subordinates		
People above you in position/ status		
People below you in position/ status		

Figure 31. Conflict management exercise worksheet.

Step 2

Most of us use different techniques for resolving conflicts with different people. Sometimes people in different situations require different techniques—you may not be able to talk to your boss the way that you talk to your best friends. But often we use a very limited number of techniques with certain people.

The Conflict-Management Exercise Worksheet (figure 31) lists various groups of people with whom you probably have occasion to interact. After each group, indicate the technique or techniques (by number from the above list of techniques) that you most frequently use to handle conflicts with them. Enter the number of the technique in the column labeled *Techniques you frequently use* on figure 31. (For example, if you often change the subject with your parents, place a 2 in the "Frequently" column after "Parents.") Disregard any groups of people with whom you do not normally interact (i.e., that do not apply to you).

Step 3

Review your responses in light of figure 32, which relates the thirty typical techniques with the classic conflict-management styles. Select responses that you would like to use with the groups or persons you selected in figure 31 and record them in the column labeled *Techniques you might use*. The techniques you select are those that you might apply effectively to improve your typical responses to conflict situations.

Technique	Collaborator 1	Compromiser 2	Accommodator 3	Controller 4	Avoider 5
1					X
2					X
3	X				
4					X
5	X				
6			X		
7			X		
8		X			
9				X	
10	X				
11		X			
12			X		
13	X				
14				X	
15		X			
16				X	
17				X	
18	X				
19				X	
20			X		
21					X
22		X			
23				X	
24					X
25		X			
26			X		
27	X				
28			X		
29		X			
30					X

Figure 32. Conflict management styles reflected by the typical conflict techniques.

Conflict Behavior Survey*

This conflict behavior survey has been designed to assist you in becoming aware of your characteristic approach or style in managing conflict. In completing this survey, you are invited to respond by making choices that correspond with your typical behavior in a particular conflict situation.

*Section I: Survey**

The survey consists of several pairs of statements describing possible behavioral responses to conflict. Please review each pair of statements and select the one that would be most characteristic of your behavior. Please circle the A or B response in the column to the right of the pair.

Please choose a single frame of reference (e.g., work-related conflicts, family conflicts, social conflicts) and keep that frame of reference in mind when responding to all the situations. And remember, as you complete this survey, that it is not a test. There are no right or wrong responses. The survey will be helpful to you only to the extent that your responses accurately represent your characteristic behavior or attitudes.

Conflict Behavior Instrument

STATEMENTS			COLUMNS			
		1	2	3	4	5
1.	A. You sometimes let the other party take responsibility for resolving the conflict.			B		(A)
	B. Rather than negotiate the issues on which you disagree, you try to stress the issues upon which you both agree.					
2.	A. You attempt to find a compromise solution to the conflict.	B	(A)			
	B. You attempt to deal with all of the other party's concerns as well as your own.					
3.	A. You are usually firm in pursuing your goals.			B	(A)	
	B. You might attempt to soothe the other party's feelings and seek to preserve your relationship.					
4.	A. You attempt to find a compromise solution to the conflict.		(A)	B		
	B. You sometimes sacrifice your own wishes for the wishes of the other party.					
5.	A. You consistently seek the other party's help in working out a solution to the conflict.	A				(B)
	B. You attempt to do what is necessary to avoid useless tension.					
	TOTAL, PAGE 107	0	2	0	1	2

*Based on Kenneth W. Thomas and Ralph H. Kilmann's *Conflict Mode Instrument,* (Tuxedo, New York: XICOM, Inc., 1974) used with permission.
*Based on Kenneth W. Thomas and Ralph H. Kilmann's *Conflict Mode Instrument,* (Tuxedo, New York: XICOM, Inc., 1974) used with permission.

STATEMENTS			COLUMNS		
	1	2	3	4	5
6. A. You attempt to avoid creating unpleasantness for yourself. B. You attempt to win your position.				(B)	A
7. A. You attempt to postpone the issue until you have had some time to think it over. B. You give up some points in exchange for others.		B			(A)
8. A. You are usually firm in pursuing your goals. B. You attempt to get all concerns and issues immediately out in the open.	B			(A)	
9. A. You feel that differences are not always worth worrying about. B. You make some effort to get your way.				(B)	A
10. A. You are usually firm in pursuing your goals. B. You attempt to find a compromise solution to the conflict.		B		(A)	
11. A. You attempt to get all concerns and issues immediately out in the open. B. You might attempt to soothe the other party's feelings and seek to preserve your relationship.	(A)		B		
12. A. You sometimes avoid taking positions which would create controversy. B. You will let the other party get some of his or her needs and interests met if you also get some of yours met.		(B)			A
13. A. You propose a middle ground. B. You press to get your points made.		A		(B)	
14. A. You tell the other party your ideas and ask for his or hers. B. You attempt to show the other party the logic and benefits of your position.	A			(B)	
15. A. You might attempt to soothe the other party's feelings and seek to preserve your relationship. B. You attempt to do what is necessary to avoid useless tensions.			A		(B)
16. A. You attempt not to hurt the other party's feelings. B. You attempt to convince the other party of the logic and benefits of your position.			A	(B)	
TOTAL, PAGE 108	1	1	0	7	2

	STATEMENTS	COLUMNS				
		1	2	3	4	5
17.	A. You are usually firm in pursuing your goals.				(A)	B
	B. You attempt to do what is necessary to avoid useless tension.					
18.	A. If it makes the other party happy, you might let him or her maintain his or her views.		(B)	A		
	B. You will let the other party get some of his or her needs and interests met if you also get some of yours met.					
19.	A. You attempt to get all concerns and issues immediately out in the open.	(A)				B
	B. You attempt to postpone the issue until you have had some time to think it over.					
20.	A. You attempt to immediately work through differences.	(A)	B			
	B. You attempt to find a fair combination of gains and losses for both you and the other party.					
21.	A. In approaching negotiations, you try to be considerate of the other party's wishes.	(B)		A		
	B. You always lean toward a direct discussion of the problem.					
22.	A. You attempt to find a position that is intermediate between the other party's position and your position.		(A)		B	
	B. You state your wishes and try to get them met at all costs.					
23.	A. You are very often concerned with satisfying everyone's wishes.	A				(B)
	B. You sometimes let the other party take responsibility for resolving the conflict.					
24.	A. If the other party's position seems very important to him or her, you would try to meet his or her wishes.		B	(A)		
	B. You attempt to get the other party to settle for a compromise.					
	TOTAL, PAGE 109	3	2	1	1	1

STATEMENTS	COLUMNS				
	1	2	3	4	5
25. A. You attempt to show the other party the logic and benefits of your positions. B. In approaching negotiations, you try to be considerate of the other party's wishes.				B	(A)
26. A. You propose a middle ground. B. You are nearly always concerned with satisfying the wishes of all parties in a conflict.	B	(A)			
27. A. You sometimes avoid taking positions that would create controversy. B. If it makes the other party happy, you might let him or her maintain his or her views.			(B)		A
28. A. You are usually firm in pursuing your goals. B. You consistently seek the other party's help in working out a solution to the conflict.	B		(A)		
29. A. You propose a middle ground. B. You feel that differences are not always worth worrying about.		A			(B)
30. A. You attempt not to hurt the other party's feelings. B. You always share the problem with the other person so that it can be mutually worked out.	B		(A)		
TOTAL, PAGE 110		1	2	1	2

Section 2: Scoring

Step 1

When you have completed all the items in Section 1, total the number of circles in each column on each page of the instrument and transfer the totals to the appropriate spaces in figure 33.

Step 2

Transfer your column total scores from figure 33 to figure 34 indicating your ideal order.

Step 3

Transfer the style names, in order of the highest ranking score first, on to figure 35, which shows your order, and enter the scores in the adjacent blank spaces.

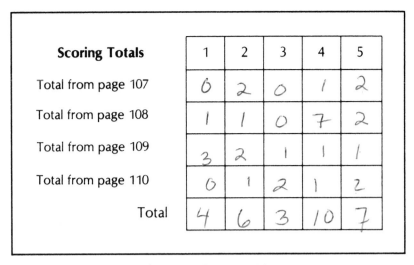

Scoring Totals	1	2	3	4	5
Total from page 107	0	2	0	1	2
Total from page 108	1	1	0	7	2
Total from page 109	3	2	1	1	1
Total from page 110	0	1	2	1	2
Total	4	6	3	10	7

Figure 33. Scoring table.

Style		Score
1. Collaborator	(Column 1)	4
2. Compromiser	(Column 2)	6
3. Accommodator	(Column 3)	3
4. Controller	(Column 4)	10
5. Avoider	(Column 5)	7
TOTAL		

Figure 34. Ideal order.

Choice	Style	Score
1st	Controller	10
2nd	Avoider	7
3rd	Compromiser	6
4th	Collaborator	4
5th	Accommodator	3
TOTAL:		

Figure 35. Your order.

Conflict Reflection Exercises

With most individuals, a particular approach or style of conflict is situational. That is, under certain circumstances or with a specific individual you might find yourself using a particular conflict style, while in a different situation, using quite another style.

111

The following two exercises are designed to assist you in identifying your conflict profile from your personal experience.

Exercise 1 Instructions

Step 1

Bring to mind a recent conflict experience in your *personal life*—who was present, who originated the conflict, what did you do, what was the response, what happened, how did you feel. Enter the information from your reflection in the space marked *Personal Conflict Experience* in Figure 36.

Step 2

Bring to mind a recent conflict experience in your *professional life*—who was present, who originated the conflict, what did you do, what was the response, what happened, how did you feel. Enter the information from your reflection in the space marked *Professional Conflict Experience* in Figure 36.

Step 3

As you score your responses to steps 1 and 2, what common themes emerge for you in terms of your patterns of settling disputes and differences. Enter the information from your reflection in the space marked *Some common themes that emerged for me* in Figure 36.

Conflict Profile Worksheet—I

Personal Conflict Experience

• What style did you use?

• How appropriate was the style to the situation?

• As you reflect on the experience now, what style would have been appropriate? Why?

Professional Conflict Experience

• What style did you use?

• How appropriate was the style to the situation?

• As you reflect on the experience now, what style would have been appropriate? Why?

Some common themes that emerged for me

Figure 36. Conflict profile worksheet.

Exercise 2 Instructions

Step 1. Bring to mind a specific situation in each of the conflict style categories noted in figure 37.

Step 2. Record who you were with; where; what was happening; what you wanted to happen; what did happen; and what you felt, thought, and did in the space provided in figure 37.

Step 3. Indicate the extent to which this example can be generalized—that is, the extent to which it typifies your behavior with respect to a particular person, a certain type of person, or a specific situation.

Conflict Profile Worksheet—II

Collaborate A time I collaborated in a conflict and arrived at a win/win outcome for myself and the other person:	
Compromise A time I compromised in a conflict when I achieved some of my outcomes but sacrificed others:	
Accommodate A time I gave up satisfying my outcome in a conflict to preserve my relationship with the other party:	
Control A time I achieved my outcome at the expense of the other person in a conflict:	
Avoid A time I avoided a conflict completely and sacrificed my outcomes as a consequence:	
Some common themes that emerged for me:	

Figure 37. Conflict profile worksheet.

Conflict-Management Skills

Conflict management, as previously indicated, is the process of becoming aware of a conflict, diagnosing its nature, and employing an appropriate methodology to diffuse the emotional energy involved and enable the disputing parties to understand and resolve their differences.

Managing conflict to achieve win/win resolutions requires two specific skills, conflict reduction and problem solving. Conflict reduction is required to reduce the emotional tension and arrive at a clear understanding of the dispute or difference. Problem solving is required to work out a solution that meets both parties desires.

The principal focus in conflict reduction is diffusing the high emotional energy involved and achieving mutual understanding of differences. Once the emotional energy is reduced and differences still remain, it is appropriate to use problem solving to achieve a win/win outcome. The basic problem solving process presented in Chapter 5 is an effective process for arriving at a resolution of the conflict satisfactory to the parties involved. Problem solving in this context is the process of identifying the discrepancy between the current and desired state and working out the specific steps required to reach a desired state that is satisfactory to all the parties involved. The Seven Step Problem Solving Process presented in Chapter 5, modified slightly for use in conflict situations is presented in figure 38 for ready reference.

Conflict can be around needs or values. A need is a primary influencer of human behavior that motivates an individual to action. Human needs are rooted in the basic physiological drive for the survival of the species. These needs change as people mature and acquire new skills. Appendix C summarizes Maslow's theory of human needs. In Maslow's system, needs are organized in a hierarchy of prepotency.

A value is something that is deeply felt by the holder, is freely chosen from alternatives, is acted upon and lived out. In their book, *Values and Teaching,* Louis Raths, Merrill Harmin and Sidney Simon defined a value in seven aspects divided into three categories: choosing, prizing, and acting.* These seven aspects or criteria serve as a working definition of a value. The seven criteria or valuing processes are:

Choosing

1. To choose freely.

2. To choose from alternatives.

3. To choose from alternatives after thoughtful consideration of the consequences of each alternative.

Seven Step Problem Solving Process
(Interpersonal Conflict Situations)

1. Define the problem in terms of both party's interests ("how to _____ statement.").
2. Identify as many options for solution as possible (brainstorm) and clarify as necessary.
3. Evaluate the options.
4. Decide on the best option or combination of options.
5. Develop implementation/action plan.
6. Include evaluation process in implementation/action plan.
7. Talk about the experience.

Figure 38. Seven step problem solving process used with interpersonal conflict situations.

---

*Louis Raths, Merrill Harmin, and Sidney Simon, *Values and Teaching* (Mellvill Publishing, Columbus, 1978), page 28.

Prizing

    4. Cherishing and being happy with the choice.

    5. Willing to affirm the choice publicly.

Acting

    6. Actually doing something with the choice.

    7. Acting repeatedly with the choice in some life pattern.

Values originate in an individuals consciousness/meaning system and are expressed in behavior. Behavior is the act of choosing at a conscious or unconscious level a person, object, relationship or process. The choice is made to satisfy a priority need which at the same time expresses a value.

Values can be divided into primary or ends values and secondary or means values. Primary values are essential to human growth. These are understood to be chosen, acted upon, and essential to the authentic development of the person. Primary core values are prerequisite to natural human development and are rooted in self respect and respect for others. Means values are those which need to be internalized to meet the primary values. These are often referred to as "skill" values.

Brian Hall* has identified 120 values which he suggests can be distributed on a developmental continuum. This continuum (Four phases in the Development of Consciousness), along with the values list and the values distributed on the continuum, are included in Appendix D.

Values are connected to skills. For any value a constellation of skills can be identified that are required in order for a person to internalize the value. For example, value, listening, sharing trust, and a number of skills are required for internalization, as shown in figure 39.

In this context, Brian Hall defines a skill as "the internalized ability to actualize a value or set of priorities . . ."** in your behavior. The skills dealt with in this book are those which enable you to establish and maintain satisfactory relationships, act with generosity and understanding toward others, get your interests met without infringing on the other, and settling disputes in win/win ways. These particular skills are essential to operationalize a Phase III level of consciousness. (Appendix D)

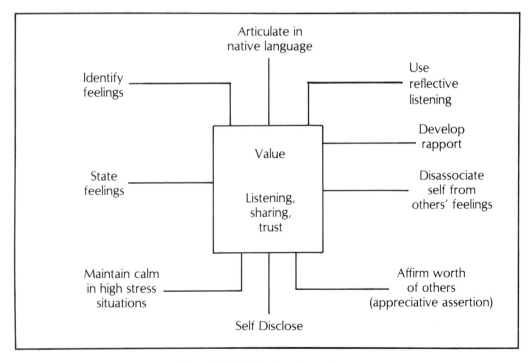

Figure 39. Skills related to values.

*Brian P. Hall, and Helen Thompson, *Leadership Through Values* (New York: Paulist Press), page 51.
**Brian P. Hall and Benjamin Tonna *God's Plan For Us* (New York: Paulist Press, 1980), page 63.

When you experience a values difference with another, you are dealing with a developmental difference that might stem from the lack of ability or willingness to engage specific skills in a particular life situation on either your or another's part. As a person with effective communication skills, it is your responsibility to acquire a flexibility necessary to elicit the response you want from another in order to get your outcome and enable the other to get his or her outcome as well.

There is a fine line distinction between needs and values—the key for conflict management purposes is to ask the question:

"Does it tangibly affect me?"

If it involves your time, property, money or health, it is most likely a need. If it is less tangible, either psychological or highly generalized, it is treated as if it is a value for conflict management purposes.

Needs Conflicts:

1. *Mutually exclusive goals*—where one goal is considered or achieved at the cost of or to the exclusion of another. This can be the case when two parties have opposing expectations or desires about their relationship.

2. *Control over scarce resources*—such as space, property, money, power, prestige, food—where two or more parties seek exclusive possession of, use of, or control over a given part of the resource. In this case, similar goals may be desired by all parties, but achievement may involve commodities that are in short supply.

3. *Means differences*—where the same end goals are desired, but the means for their attainment are perceived differently.

Values Conflicts:

4. *Values*—where two or more parties disagree on what "should be." It is not the value per se that leads to the conflict but rather the claim that one value should dominate or be applied generally, even to those who hold different values.

5. *Beliefs*—where two or more parties disagree over what "is," such as facts, information, knowledge, or beliefs about reality.

6. *Preferences*—where the tastes of two or more parties impinge on each others' preferences, sensitivities, or sensibilities.

Although each conflict situation involves differing dynamics, structure, and role definitions, most interpersonal conflicts can be considered as either conflicts of *needs* or conflicts of *values,* as shown above. The conflict involved may be either real or perceived.

Conflict of needs grows out of similarities in the needs, personal goals, and aspirations of parts of a system in the presence of scarce and undistributable goods. Two siblings desiring the same toy are experiencing a conflict of needs, as are companies trying to reach the same market. Enlarging the supply of the scarce goods may minimize or resolve the conflict. Changing the image of the resource desired (love, money) to joint utilization rather than sole possession might resolve the conflict by lifting it to a higher level of cooperation. Problem solving is usually required to resolve this type of conflict.

Conflict of values grows out of differences in values among parts of a system. This is ideological conflict, where contention is rooted in perceived differences in norms, values, and beliefs, accompanied by strong feelings. The values of one part of a system, for example, may favor one direction of movement over another. Then again, differences may lie not in direction but in the methods favored to reach the goal, where people have no interest other than defending their own system of values. To defend one's own value system without attacking another's is a difficult skill. All parties must focus on utilizing their differences in a common quest for shared goals and real solutions. Conflicts of needs often underlie conflicts of values so problem solving is often required to resolve the situation.

Conflict Outcomes

Conflict may have a number of outcomes, depending on the approach the opposing parties use to manage it. The conflict may result in *resentment,* because one side has gained a complete victory, a frozen stalemate has occurred, or both sides have agreed to a compromise with which neither is satisfied; or it may result in *mutual respect,* because both sides have participated in developing a creative new solution with which both are satisfied. The question in conflict management is how to achieve the outcome of mutual respect, for only then can conflict be constructive and growth-producing.

Now let's take a look at some of the typical conflict-management styles that were discussed earlier in light of the outcomes they produce in a relationship. To briefly review, the styles are:

- *Collaborator*—the *win/win* posture, in which the collaborator seeks to maintain a strong interpersonal relationship while ensuring that both parties to the conflict achieve their personal goals.

- *Compromiser*—The *mini-win/mini-lose* posture, in which the compromiser assumes that a mutually satisfactory (win/win) solution cannot be achieved and instead tries to win as much as possible while preserving the interpersonal relationship as much as possible.

- *Accommodator*—the *yield-lose/win* posture, in which the accommodator tries above all to protect the interpersonal relationship with the opposing party, conceding his or her own goals in the process.

- *Controller*—the *win/lose* posture, in which the controller seeks to have his or her personal goals met, regardless of any damage that may be done to the relationship with the opposing party.

- *Avoider*—the *leave-lose/win* posture, in which the avoider shuns conflict itself, conceding both his or her own goals and the relationship with the opposing party rather than confront the issue.

The *win/win* approach to conflict management is one in which the problem is viewed as external to the persons involved, and the opposing parties collaborate to seek a high-quality solution that meets their mutual needs while preserving their relationship. The win/win style involves the use of true problem-solving methods and is generally the ideal approach for managing both conflicts of needs and conflicts of values, since it results in mutual respect between the conflicting parties.

The other styles of conflict management—which, as a group, are sometimes called *forcing styles*—are those in which each party tackles the problem separately, with the problem coming between the parties and distancing them, and with one or both parties ending up settling for a solution that does not meet their personal goals or needs. The forcing styles generally represent less-than-optimal methods for managing conflicts, since they result in resentment, which continues to distance the opposing parties.

In any relationship, there is an underlying level of emotional energy (that is, an underlying perception of resentment or mutual respect). In a relationship characterized by underlying resentment—that is, by the presence of destructive emotional energy (the level of which can vary)—the parties are predisposed to engage in conflict, with the conflicts that do occur tending to be intense. Resentment can be thought of as unexpressed conflict, which causes feelings of distance between the parties involved. Such feelings often result from:

- Use of inappropriate conflict-management strategies.
- Anticipation of future clashes.
- Outward behavior that causes tension.
- Unexpressed apathy or indifference.
- Unsettled grievances that have accumulated over time.
- Power building by one or both parties.
- Stereotyping by one or both parties.

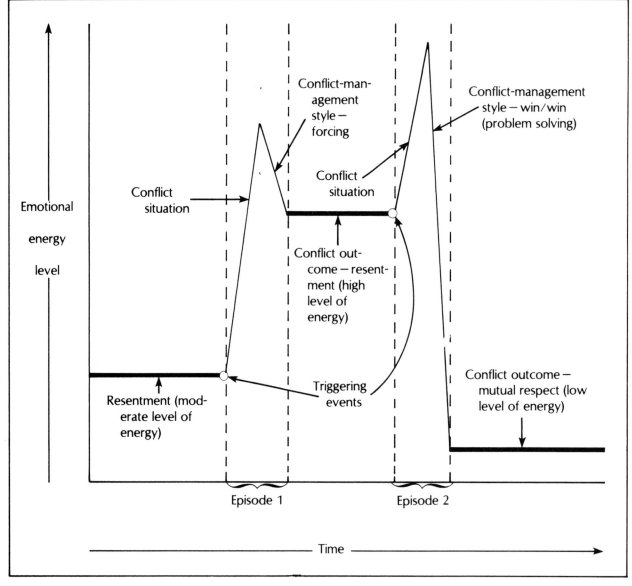

Figure 40. Conflict cycle.

In a relationship characterized by underlying mutual respect—that is, by an absence of destructive emotional energy—the parties have little or no inclination to engage in conflict, with the conflicts that do occur tending not to be intense. Such a situation is characterized by:

- Use of conflict management strategies as conflicts are recognized.
- Open expression of thoughts and feelings.
- Anticipation of the other's needs.
- Acknowledgement and appreciation of the other's positive behavior.
- Respect for diversity and individual differences.

Figure 40 illustrates part of a conflict cycle, consisting of two episodes of conflict in a relationship. As can be seen from the graph, the level of emotional energy in the relationship is at first moderately high, indicating a moderate level of resentment. The emergence of open conflict in each episode begins with a "triggering event"—a precipitating occurrence that shifts the balance of power or changes a situation either internally (change in feelings) or externally (changes in role or in pressure from the environment). The conflict situations themselves are overt expressions of conflict, involving specific instances

118

of infringement, high energy, and expressed strong feelings, resulting in a distancing of the parties involved. The significant difference between the two episodes lies in how they are managed.

The first conflict episode is handled using a forcing style, which indeed suppresses the open conflict but results in a considerably higher level of emotional energy than existed at first—that is, a higher level of underlying resentment in the relationship. The relationship is therefore even riper for a subsequent episode of conflict, which promptly breaks out following another triggering event.

The second conflict episode, in contrast, is handled using a win/win (problem-solving) style, which results in lowering the level of emotional energy in the relationship—that is, a high level of mutual respect. Use of this win/win style, then, not only results in suppression of the overt manifestations of the conflict but alters the nature of the relationship itself, such that future conflicts are much less likely to occur, and those conflicts that do occur are much less likely to be intense.

In the following subsections, we will take a closer look at the forcing and win/win styles and examine how they produce their characteristic outcomes of resentment and mutual respect before discussing the broader implications of these styles in social situations.

Forcing Styles = Resentment

Figure 41 illustrates how the forcing strategies that can be used in an attempt to settle a conflict result in resentment of one party toward the other (or of both parties toward each other). In all cases, the problem tends to come between the parties, while each tackles the problem individually. But when each party seeks his or her own solution to the problem (rather than engaging in a joint effort to discover a mutually acceptable solution), whatever solution is finally arrived at will be likely to meet the needs of only one—or neither—of the parties. The party (or parties) who have lost such a conflict as a result of a forcing strategy then harbor lingering feelings of resentment—feelings that will negatively affect the relationship and heighten chances for subsequent conflict.

The following conditions are generally associated with the forcing styles:

1. Both parties assume that one's gain necessitates the other's loss. (Each seeks the other's defeat so that the gain will be one-sided.)

2. Forcing entails the imposition of goals, methods, rules, and values.

3. Strategic considerations are aimed at defeating the opponent.

4. Since resources are viewed as fixed and limited, each party is anxious to obtain the maximum share.

5. Interaction between the two parties is governed by real or perceived power balances.

6. Each party attempts to maximize its relative ability to reward or punish the other by exercising control over information, money, formal authority, or desired associations.

7. Energies of the parties are directed against each other rather than against the common problem.

8. The content of the conflict becomes generalized from a specific issue to an atmosphere of bitter dispute.

9. Offensive and defensive strategies replace facts and reason.

10. Parties assume fixed positions to emphasize the most obvious or accessible solution rather than actually defining the problem.

11. Parties communicate with each other in ways that are judgmental and accusative rather than factual.

12. Differences between the two parties, rather than similarities, are emphasized, with denial of similarities that do exist.

13. Each party distorts the image of the other to justify his or her own right to conquest.

14. The controlling individual will characterize the controlled as uninformed, weak, childlike, or dependent.

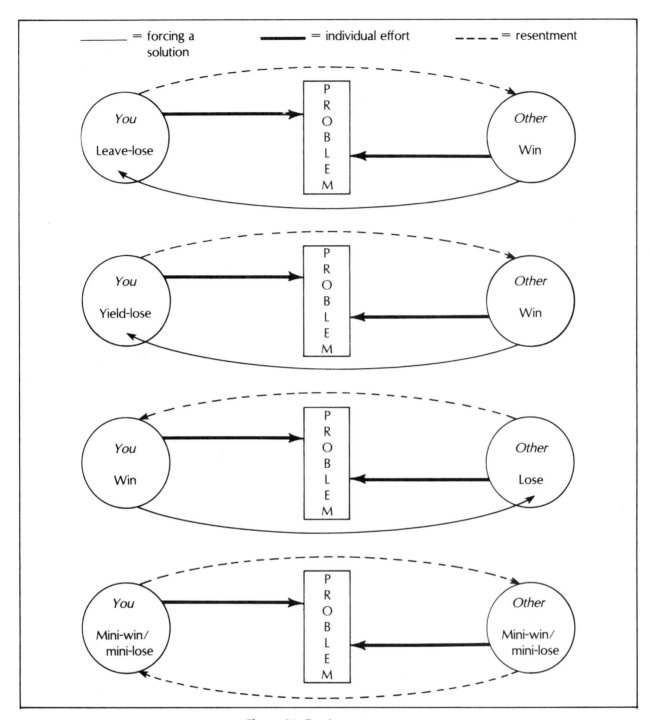

Figure 41. Forcing outcomes.

15. The needs, feelings, and attitudes of the opposition are ignored to avoid identification with his or her position.

16. The parties tend to view neutrals and moderates with the presumption that "if you are not with me, you must be against me."

17. Manipulation, threats, bluffs, etc., are used to defeat the opponent.

18. While each party accurately understands his or her own needs, the parties may publicly disguise or misrepresent those needs.

19. The parties employ unpredictable, varying strategies that involve the element of surprise.

20. Each party's search behavior is devoted to finding ways to make it look as if he or she were committed to a position, with both nonrational and irrational arguments used to support this aim.

21. Each party often tries to enhance his or her success by forming bad stereotypes of the other party's logic or behavior, or by increasing the level of hostility.

22. The forcing strategy ends when one party capitulates or manifests no further overt opposition, or when a deadlock occurs.*

In summary, the characteristics associated with forcing styles are that:

1. A clear "me/other" distinction between the parties exists, rather than a "we-versus-the-problem" orientation.

2. Each party sees the issue only from his or her own viewpoint, rather than defining the problem in terms of mutual needs.

3. The emphasis in the process is upon attainment of a predetermined solution, rather than upon defining goals, values, or benefits to be achieved with the solution.

4. Conflicts are personalized via a subjective focus on the parties involved, rather than being de-personalized via an objective focus on the facts and issues.

5. The parties are conflict-oriented emphasizing the immediate disagreement, rather than relationship-oriented emphasizing the long-term effects of whether—and how—their differences are resolved.

Win/Win Style = Mutual Respect

Figure 42 illustrates how the win/win strategy that can be used to manage a conflict results in mutual respect between the opposing parties. In contrast to forcing strategies—characterized by each party's tackling the problem individually, with the problem coming between them—the win/win approach involves both parties' objectively distancing themselves from the problem and collaborating in a joint alliance to defeat it (rather than to defeat each other). This search for a mutually acceptable solution means that both parties to the conflict win—that is, both get their personal goals or needs met. The parties

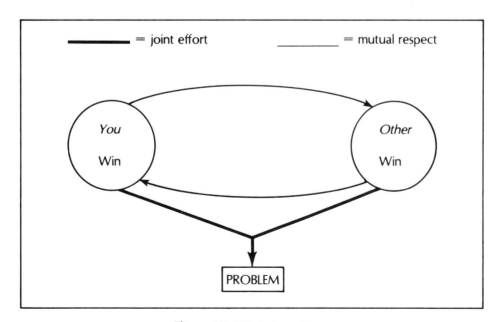

Figure 42. Win/win outcome.

*Based on Alan C. Filley, *Interpersonal Conflict Resolution* (Glenview, Ill.: Scott Foresman and Company, 1975), p. 25.

121

who win such a conflict as a result of the win/win strategy will experience feelings of mutual respect—feelings that will strengthen the relationship and lessen chances for subsequent conflict.

The following conditions are generally associated with the win/win, collaborative style:

1. Both parties assume it is possible to arrive at a high-quality solution that is mutually acceptable.
2. The parties see resources as abundant and have a common interest in finding an acceptable solution.
3. The energies of the parties are directed toward defeating the problem.
4. The content of discussions is maintained at a specific, descriptive level of interaction.
5. Both facts, opinions, and personal feelings are reported openly, and feedback is given to others without accusation or judgment.
6. Areas of agreement and disagreement are clarified.
7. Trust levels are high, permitting mutual influence through open reporting of facts and feelings.
8. Every attempt is made to ensure that all information is shared and that all information shared is accurate.
9. Particular attention is given to clarifying the problem and ensuring that all alternatives are considered before selection of a final solution takes place.
10. The parties interact freely with each other in nonhierarchical patterns.
11. The parties' behavior is purposeful in pursuing goals that both have in common.
12. The parties accurately understand their own needs, and their public behavior is a true reflection of those needs.
13. Strategies are predictable, and when flexible behavior is utilized, it is appropriate and not something designed to take the other party by surprise.
14. The parties refrain from using threats, bluffs, and manipulation.
15. Search behavior is devoted to finding solutions to problems by using logical and innovative means.
16. The parties realize that true success demands that stereotypes be dropped; that ideas be given consideration on their merits, regardless of where the ideas came from; and that hostility not be provoked or increased deliberately.
17. Dominating and yielding behavior, as well as mechanisms that avoid confronting the facts (voting, trading, resorting to rules), are avoided.
18. Similarities between the two parties, rather than differences, are identified and emphasized.
19. Neutrals and moderates are seen as potential mediators.
20. The problem-solving strategy ends when the parties reach a high-quality solution to which both are committed.*

In summary, the characteristics associated with the win/win style are that:

1. A clear "we-versus-the-problem" orientation exists between the parties, rather than a "me/other" distinction.
2. Each party defines the problem in terms of mutual needs and interests.
3. The emphasis in the process is upon defining goals, values, or benefits to be achieved with the solution, rather than upon the attainment of a solution predetermined by one or both parties.
4. Conflicts are depersonalized via an objective focus on the facts and issues, rather than being personalized via a subjective focus on the parties involved.
5. The parties are relationship-oriented emphasizing the long-term effects of whether—and how—their differences are resolved, rather than conflict-oriented, focusing on the immediate disagreement.

*Based on Alan C. Filley, *Interpersonal Conflict Resolution* (Glenview, Ill.: Scott Foresman and Company, 1975), p. 25.

Forcing and Win/Win Social Situations

Earlier in the chapter we stated that the win/win approach to managing conflict is generally preferable, since it involves combining the parties' efforts to find a mutually acceptable solution, thereby generating respect; and that the forcing approaches are generally not preferable, since they involve the parties' tackling the problem individually, with each attempting to impose his or her own solution, or with both accepting a mutually unsatisfactory solution, thereby generating resentment. That statement, however, was qualified as being only "generally" true.

You will, of course, realize that there are certain social situations that inherently lend themselves to forcing strategies rather than win/win and vice versa. The serious poker game is an example of a forcing social situation: Collaboration is ruled out, and both sides cannot entirely satisfy their goals. A buyer's interaction with a used-car dealer will also mainly be a forcing situation. Two people working together on a jigsaw puzzle, on the other hand, is an example of a win/win situation. The nature of the task lends itself to collaboration and to satisfaction of mutual needs. Discussions with a fellow team member may also largely be a win/win process.

In any interpersonal situation (relations with family, friends, on the job, etc.), two things happen as the behavior of the involved parties shifts from a forcing to a win/win approach:

1. The parties involved make the rational discovery that achieving personal goals is largely a win/win process. This fact is often not recognized at first. In the early life of a family, class, or group, many people act as if there were only a limited amount of attention, prominence, control, or influence, and they hurry to get their share. During this initial period, then, some of the involved parties relax and interact freely, while others hold back and try to gain an advantage.

   The paradox here is that as long as no one involved in the situation will accept another person's influence, there is *no* influence, and no one will be able to satisfy his or her need to be influential. Later on in the interaction, when the participants involved have stopped competing for influence, members of the group can cooperate to improve the well-being and effectiveness of the entire organization or system.

2. Emotional adjustments are also made among the members, which result in a decreased personal need to "prove oneself" or to "defeat" another.

   As long as members of a family, class, or group are hung up with competition for attention and control, very little genuine concern by anyone for anyone can develop or be shown. Mutual relationships of confidence and concern are essential to the growth of everyone involved in interpersonal situations.

Both forcing and win/win approaches can be seen operating at the same time in many interpersonal situations. For example, several people on an athletic team may be potential candidates for a key position. All are aware that they are competing for the assignment and that one will get it. Clearly, a reward structure exists that encourages forcing behavior; that is, the situation itself at least partly calls for forcing. Other aspects of the team situation, however, may demand that the same people cooperate. In this case, the involved parties have to play both the forcing and win/win games simultaneously.

Another example of how the forcing and win/win approaches may both be operating in a particular situation would be the case of a teenage girl discussing with her widowed mother the hourly wage her mother will pay the girl for performing a large number of chores around their house during the summer. On the one hand, the teenager, who will be giving up a regular summer job to do this work at home, must try to keep the hourly wage as high as possible, since she has been using money from various "odd jobs" to pay for her clothing and general expenses and save for college. On the other hand, she is well aware of how urgent it is to get the painting, mowing, minor repairs, and other chores done over the summer and knows that her mother cannot afford to hire help from outside the family to perform this work. In this case, for the daughter to approach the issue of her hourly wage entirely from a win/win standpoint would be to risk not getting paid enough to meet her personal needs. Yet for the teenager to approach the wage issue entirely from a forcing standpoint would be to ignore whatever possibilities there might be to get her own outcomes met without causing her mother to make the excessive sacrifice of either letting the chores go entirely undone or paying more than she can really afford to have them done.

Frequently, in conflict situations, a single approach is overused. One person may approach every situation as if it were a forcing game and transform every discussion into a debate, while another may approach every situation as if it were a win/win game and transform every discussion into a search for mutual goals. The appropriate choice is to see the objective reality of each situation and choose approaches that are appropriate to the specific situation. The first type of attitude might be referred to as cynical, the second naive, and the third realistic.

The cynical approach, however, in which people characteristically react to situations as if they required forcing strategies even when they do not, is common in many interactions. Often, when competition, differing priorities, and opposing goals are emphasized, the parties involved ignore whatever win/win possibilities may exist in the situation. Needlessly playing a forcing game has numerous negative consequences, each of which makes it more difficult to manage the conflict.

When the forcing approach is used, the attention of the involved parties is focused on their differences. The belief predominates that "if you are not with me, you must be against me," and the parties to the conflict place great pressure on neutrals and moderates (who are often in the best position to resolve the conflict) to take sides with one party or the other. Each party easily focuses interpersonal hostility on the other. Personalities, not issues, become the center of concern. It seems clear that this type of behavior only serves to harden the positions of both parties, preventing communication and the formation of trust, which are so vital for legitimate problem solving.

A related aspect of forcing situations is that when old and long-hidden problems are left unresolved, they often have lingering aftereffects, which surface repeatedly to influence people's perceptions of new problems and issues. In such cases, people tend to regard and approach the new issue or problem as a continuation of the previous one rather than seeing it as a separate matter. These unrealistic preconceived assumptions about conflict that people often fall into stem from underlying resentment and are called "conflict traps." Unfortunately, such conflict traps and the split between "me" and "the other" seem to be self-perpetuating and reinforcing because of the reciprocal nature of human interaction (that is, because people tend to demonstrate "tit-for-tat" behavior). If, for instance, you believe that the other party is incompetent, you tend to act as if he or she were and emphasize and exaggerate any errors the other does make. This, of course, increases the other's hostility, which just reinforces your original beliefs about him or her.

The influence of people's motivations on their perceptions of reality is another important consideration in conflict situations. It is easy to see how people attribute evil intentions to their opponents. Individuals or groups under competitive pressure nearly always enhance the value of their own efforts and downplay the efforts of others. As a consequence, any viewpoints the individuals or groups may share in common are likely to go unrecognized. Identifying defensively with your own position (i.e., withdrawing into your "shell") tends to make you feel secure and powerful, but it is a false feeling, which cuts off real interaction with the other party and can prevent you from considering the true basis for your conflict.

In situations where certain third parties such as judges or arbitrators try to step in and resolve the conflict, a different set of consequences occurs. In such cases, decisions are often made, but the conflict itself remains unresolved and tends to arise again. This tendency can be seen by examining the typical reactions of the "winners" and the "losers" when an outside judge has issued a ruling in an attempt to "settle" a conflict:

- The *winners* of such a decision are elated: they knew they were right all along. They evaluate the judge as fair and impartial. Yet they have set a precedent, and they can later be trapped by the same system of conflict resolution that gave them their victory in this case. In the long run, the victory might actually decrease the winners' ability to adapt to new problems.

- The *losers* of this type of decision, on the other hand, appear to go through two stages (besides the immediate reaction of rejecting the judge as unfair). They tend first to deny the reality of losing and try to prove that their own solutions were superior. Then they become concerned with how to win "next time," thus setting up a forcing orientation (a conflict trap) long before the next conflict has even arisen.

From this description of conflict patterns, it becomes easy to see how people's judgments and perceptions get distorted and how conflict arises when emotions and motives are not recognized. This insight offers a valuable clue to how conflict can be studied when attempting to diagnose problems in a particular setting. If you and the other party involved reexamine a disagreement, you may discover that no real conflict of goals or competitive reward structure exists. Instead, if you could deal with many of the non-rational forces, the win/win possibilities might begin to emerge. For instance, the basic attitudes underlying the interpersonal relations between the two individuals might be what is preventing cooperation rather than a disagreement over the issue itself. In that case, a productive approach would be for the involved parties to spend some time and effort working directly on improving interpersonal relations, or for the reality of the issue or problem to be presented objectively to the parties and mutual trust, respect, and concern developed between them.

If a conflict is identified and determined not to be based on the misconceptions or illogical fears of the parties involved, then a major step will have been taken toward resolving it, because conflict based in *fact* is the easiest kind of conflict to manage effectively. In reality, however, there are probably few pure cases; most conflicts present a mixture of unrealistic and realistic perceptions, attitudes, and expectations.

Position vs. Interests

Distinguishing between position and interests is essential for effective conflict management. Roger Fisher and William Ury make the distinction clearly in their work *Getting to Yes,** as follows:

- Position: What you decided you want in a dispute or difference—a particular solution.
- Interest: What caused you to decide—your specific needs in the dispute or difference that caused you to take a particular position or arrive at a particular solution.

Your position is essentially a specific solution that will meet your outcome. Underlying your position are your interests. It is your interests, your fundamental needs in a situation, that usually cause you to arrive at a specific solution.

A conflict with another is usually around positions. When people "lock into" positions the best outcome possible is a compromise. The possibility for achieving a win/win outcome in a dispute and differences emerge because of the commonality of interests of the parties. This commonality promotes dovetailing the interests (outcomes) to achieve a resolution to the conflict that is satisfying and pleasing to the parties involved.

Conflict-Management Process

The conflict-management process normally begins with one party invading or infringing on the psychological, physical, or value territory of another. The conflict-management model presented in this book and pictured in figure 43 involves five stages, as follows:

Stage 1

Awareness. This stage, involving the parties' coming to awareness of a struggle, is the first sign of perceived conflict. It emerges around the awareness of incompatible needs or values, usually because of:

- An assertion, where one party asserts to another party or parties.
- Where one party takes a stand on an issue that is opposed by another party or parties.
- Feedback, where one party gives feedback to another and the feedback is resisted.

Stage 2

Diagnosis. This stage involves the parties' understanding whether the conflict is one of needs or values. The key to whether the conflict involves needs or values at its roots is "Does the conflict have tangible and concrete consequences for the parties," that is, does it affect the time, property, money, or health of the disputants?

*Based on Roger Fisher and William Ury, *Getting to Yes* (Boston: Houghton Mifflin, 1981).

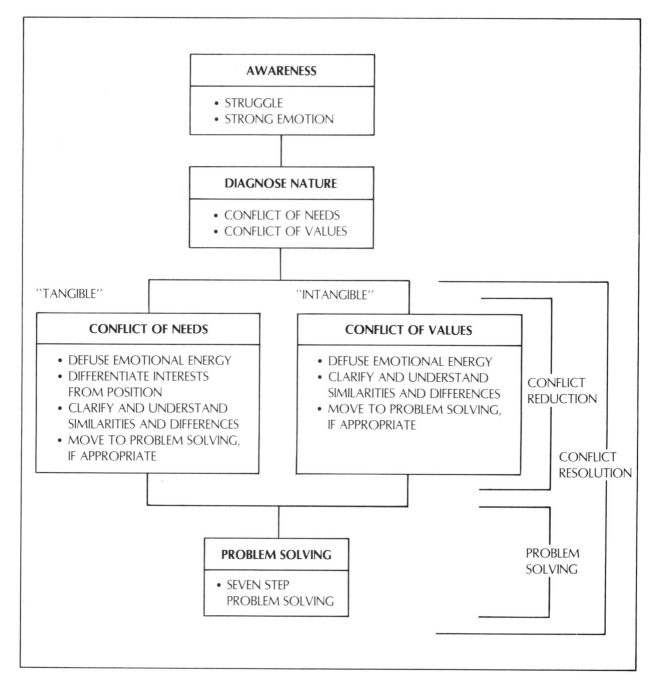

Figure 43. Conflict-management model.

Stage 3

Conflict reduction. This stage involves reducing the level of emotional energy (defusing negative emotions) and clarifying and understanding differences so that the disputing parties can settle the conflict—that is, agree to reduce destructive behavior as well as negative attitudes and feelings toward each other. This settlement may not be an agreement that resolves all the differences but one that enables both parties to go forward with an understanding of differences and mutual respect for each other.

Stage 4

Problem solving. This stage involves engaging in a problem solving process to uncover a course of action that will satisfy the principal interests of all parties to a conflict and completely resolve the conflict situation.

This conflict management process is predicated on the following principles of conflict management:

- The essence of conflict is the high emotional energy around perceived differences.
- The essence of conflict reduction is the diffusion of the high emotional energy and mutual understanding of differences.
- Resolution of the conflict often involves problem solving to bring about a win/win outcome.
- The keys to effective conflict management are:
  —Reflective listening to insure understanding.
  —Maintaining rapport at all times.
  —Differentiating position from interests.
  —Working toward a win/win outcome through dovetailing interests.
- The essence of conflict is the emotional energy around perceived differences.
- The essence of conflict management is the diffusion of the emotional energy.
- Resolution often involves negotiating the differences for win/win outcomes (dovetailing interests).

The following provides a brief introductory overview of the two conflict reduction strategies which will enable you to compare their main features: a five-step method for conflicts of needs and a seven-step method for conflicts of values.

Five Step Method
(conflicts of needs)

1. Listen to the other's position using reflective listening skills.
2. Re-state your position and identify the interests which underlie it.
3. Elicit the other's interests.
4. Summarize and gain agreement on the similarities and differences in interests.
5. Move to problem solving, if appropriate.

Seven Step Method
(conflicts of values)

1. Listen to the other's position using reflective listening skills.
2. Summarize the other's view to his or her satisfaction.
3. Invite the other to hear your view.
4. State your view.
5. Ask the other to summarize your view to your satisfaction.
6. Summarize and gain agreement on similarities and differences (repeat steps 1 through 5, as appropriate).
7. Move to problem solving, if appropriate.

Both the conflict reduction and problem solving strategies are based on the following assumptions:

- People have the resources to make the changes they wish to make.
- People are doing the best they can at any particular moment in time.
- A mutually acceptable solution is available and is desirable (i.e., shared needs or goals).
- Cooperation is preferable to competition.
- The views openly expressed by others are perceived by them to be legitimate representations of their true positions.
- The existence of differing opinions is helpful.
- The other party is capable of competing but has freely chosen to cooperate.

The win/win option, in short, is an assertive approach to conflict. As we shall see in the following subsections, it both requires and builds mutual respect and fosters the self-respect of the parties involved in a conflict.

Managing Conflicts of Needs

A need is a primary influencer of human behavior that motivates an individual to action. Conflicts of needs emerge when the wants and positions taken by the parties involved are perceived to be mutually opposing and interfere with one another in some way. Needs are concrete and tangible, usually involving your time, property, money or health.

Essential to managing conflicts of needs is differentiating position from interests. As pointed out in the subsection on conflict management, your position is what you decided you want, your interests are what caused you to decide that particular position. Your interests answer the question, "Why did you choose that particular position?"

For example, Jack decided to sell his ten year old car for $9,000, a price he chose by examining the asking price for similar cars in the newspaper. A buyer answered Jack's advertisement and offered him $7,000 for the car. The positions of the two parties were:

Jack's position—$9,000.00

Potential buyer's position—$7,000.00

A compromise might be to split the difference at $8,000, but this would likely result in some feelings of resentment on both sides. Jack decided that a win/win outcome is wiser and entered into a conflict management strategy to achieve an outcome satisfactory to both parties. Jack then reflected on the situation and identified his interests and elicited the potential buyers interests. The interests of the two parties were:

Jack's Interests

1. A price that is just and fair.
2. Get the money on delivery of the car in order to purchase another one.
3. Have the potential buyer satisfied so that the potential buyer would not bother Jack in the future.

Potential Buyer's Interests

1. A price that is just and fair.
2. Get the car right away ttake a trip.
3. Get the repair records to verify the maintenance history.

As Jack and the potential buyer surveyed the interests, both agreed to *all* the interests. The only hitch was what is just and fair. The two decided to use the N.A.D.A. Used Car Guide to determine a just and fair price by splitting the difference between the retail and wholesale value for the make and year of the car. Both parties were happy at a price of $8,400. No feelings of resentment remained.

Needs conflicts are managed by first using the following five step conflict reduction process:

1. *Listen to the other's position using reflective listening skills*—when the other expresses a differing position, opinion or stand, let him or her know you have heard by reflecting the ideas and feelings accurately and to the other's satisfaction. Get rapport and maintain it at all times during the process.

2. *Restate your position and identify the interests which underlie it*—restate your position, pointing out the similarities and differences, and then identify your interests. In this way you can explain and demonstrate how to differentiate position from interest.

3. *Elicit the other's interests*—when you have finished identifying your interests invite the other to surface his or her interests. Carefully reflective listen to the other's interests and help him or her clarify them. Point out the similarities and differences in interests. Remember to maintain rapport.

4. *Summarize and gain agreement on the differences in interests*—when both party's interests have been stated and clarified, summarize them identifying which, if any, require objective criteria for getting agreement. If any do:
   - Frame each issue as a joint search for objective criteria.
   - Be open to which standards would be most appropriate and how they should be applied.
   - Never yield to pressure, only to principle.*

*Roger Fisher and William Ury, *Getting to Yes* (New York: Penguin Books, 1984), page 91.

5. *Move to problem solving, if appropriate*—often the conflict can be resolved easily once the underlying interests have been identified. When differences in interests remain, invite the other to problem solve using the seven step problem solving process. If problem solving is indicated, develop a problem statement that encompasses both party's interests.

The seven step problem solving method can be used by parties involved in a conflict of needs in an attempt to arrive at a solution that meets the interests of both. The process is as follows:

1. Define the problem in terms of both persons' interests.
2. Identify as many options for solution as possible and clarify options that are ambiguous.
3. Evaluate the options.
4. Decide on the best option or combination of options.
5. Develop an implementation plan (decide who will do what and when).
6. Develop a process for evaluating the effectiveness of the solution.
7. Talk about the experience.

The use of the seven step process listed above results in an appropriate action plan for attending to the problem. Future steps would include implementing the agreed-upon solution and evaluating the results in accordance with the action plan.

Guidelines for Using the Seven Step Problem Solving Method

1. *Define the problem in terms of the interests of both parties:*
   - State the problem in a way that does not communicate blame or judgment.
   - Test out the problem statement and gain acceptance.
   - Maintain rapport at all times.
   - Reflective listen to the other.
   - Be sure you understand the other's interests and be ready to clarify yours, as needed.
   - Be congruent.
   - Take your time.
2. *Identify (and clarify) all possible options for solution:*
   - Ask the other to suggest possible solutions.
   - Use reflective listening; treat the other's ideas with respect.
   - Discourage evaluation until a number of possible options have been proposed.
3. *Evaluate options for solution:*
   - Be honest.
   - Use reflective listening.
   - Be open to new options and modifications that come to mind.
   - Test any likely options to make sure they satisfy both parties' needs.
4. *Decide on an acceptable solution:*
   - Don't push or impose a solution on the other.
   - When a decision appears close, state this so that both understand it.
5. *Develop an implementation plan:*
   - Decide specifically who does what and when.
6. *Develop a process for evaluating effectiveness:*
   - Incorporate this process into the implementation plan.

7. *Talk about the experience:*
  - Invite the other to share perspectives on the process.
  - Share your own perspectives on the process.

Important Points to Remember in Problem Solving

- Invite the other to use the problem-solving method.
- Describe the process in one sentence.
- Ask permission to take notes.
- Maintain rapport at all times.
- Be assertive with your position and interests naturally and directly.
- Reflective listen to help the other get interests stated and met.
- Write down every solution suggested in brainstorming.
- Be open to unusual solutions.
- Don't settle for a solution that doesn't meet the interests of both parties.
- Respond to your own emotional reactions during the process. Be sensitive to those of the other.
- Be genuine and express respect and empathy.

Suggestions for Breaking Deadlocks

- Go back to brainstorming to generate additional options.
- Go back to the definition of needs and attempt to redefine the problem. There may be an underlying issue that is not being addressed.
- Make a direct appeal to the other party—e.g., "Can you figure out why we are having trouble finding an acceptable solution? What is blocking us?"
- See if the other would be willing to sleep on the problem or reflect on it and resume later.
- Ask if more study, more data, or additional facts are needed.
- Call in an outside consultant.
- Inform the other of the consequences of failure to meet time constraints if there are sufficient reasons why a solution must be reached immediately.
- See if the other would be willing to try out one of the proposed solutions for a period of time.

What the Problem Solving Approach Communicates

Each step of the problem solving approach, as it is used with another person, in conflict situations conveys unspoken messages that can and often do reach the other. Each of these messages is mutually affirming and increases the feeling of common respect and concern for the outcomes in the relationship.

STEP	MESSAGE
1. DEFINING THE PROBLEM IN TERMS OF INTERESTS	Both you and your interests are important to me. I am important enough to express my needs and have them heard. We really can understand each another.
2. GENERATING ALL POSSIBLE OPTIONS FOR SOLUTION BEFORE EVALUATING	I value your creative thinking as well as my own and believe that by joining forces we can increase our creativity.
3. EVALUATING THE SOLUTIONS	I want to have both your interests and my interests satisfied and won't accept either one of us suppressing our individual differences.

4. DECIDING ON A SOLUTION	You have the power to change the situation you are in and significant control over your own life space. I, likewise, have control of my situation and the power to change it.
5. PLANNING FOR IMPLEMENTATION	You have power, and I have power. Together we can achieve more than either of us alone.
6. DEVELOPING A PROCESS FOR EVALUATING THE EFFECTIVENESS OF THE SOLUTION	We are not locked into any position, solution, policy, or program but have the power to continually revise and improve it.
7. TALKING ABOUT THE EXPERIENCE	Evaluation has value, and we can therefore profit from a review of the process in which we are engaged.

Problem Solving Role-Plays

To enhance your understanding of the seven step method of problem solving conflicts of needs, the following role-play situations are included in this subsection:

Situations	Skilled Roles	Unskilled Roles
The Graduate Student Dilemma	Graduate Student	Professor
The Basketball Dilemma	Professor	Student
The Workload Dilemma	Administrator	Volunteer
The "Walkman" Dilemma	Customer	Store Owner
The Dog Dilemma	Neighbor	Owner
The Library Dilemma	Student	Head Librarian

Each of the role-play dilemmas presented below involves an encounter between an individual who possesses effective listening, assertion, and problem solving skills (the "skilled" roles) and another who does not possess such skills (the "unskilled" roles). In each role-play, the problem or issue involved is described from *two* perspectives: that of the skilled party and that of the unskilled party. In order to make this role-play exercise more reflective of real-life communication situations, do try when reading the description of your own role not to "peek" at the description of the role of the person with whom you will be in conflict.

Before turning to the role-plays, please familiarize yourself with the following sets of guidelines.

Directions for Those Playing the Skilled Roles:

1. Reflective listen.
2. Maintain rapport at all times.
3. Try to identify the other person's interests.
4. Define the problem in terms of both party's interests (e.g., "As I see it, our problem is that your interests are to _____ , and my interests are _____").
5. Write down alternative options. Don't evaluate until all options have been offered.
6. Don't settle for a solution that would not meet your needs.
7. Respond to your feelings during this process.
8. Be open to far-out solutions if they meet your interests.

Directions for Those Playing the Unskilled Roles:

1. Modify your role depending on the behavior or message of the other person.
2. Don't prolong the role-playing by being rigidly resistant; yet don't accept solutions that do not meet your needs.
3. Be in touch with changes in your own gut feelings during the problem-solving process rather than trying single-mindedly to "play the part."

The Graduate Student Dilemma

Graduate Student's Role (Skilled): You are John Smith, a part-time graduate student at a local university. You are now in the middle of the semester, and you decide you must have a conference with your economics professor, Dr. James, to talk about the final examination.

You enjoy economics and you have done a lot of outside reading and have participated actively in the class discussions. However, you know that this professor's final examination is always objective (True-False). This scares you, because for some reason you always do poorly on such examinations. You do well on essay tests and you write excellent term papers. You know that your grade will suffer if you are required to take the objective final examination. Based on the grades you have received on papers and essay tests, you should receive an A in the course.

Your position is to convince Dr. James to excuse you from the final or allow you to demonstrate to him that you know the material of the course by some means other than the objective final examination. You have scheduled a meeting with Dr. James.

Your interests in this situation are:

1. You wish to show the professor you have mastered the material.
2. You want to maintain your good relationship with the professor.
3. You want to do well in the course.

Professor's Role (Unskilled): You are Professor James, an economics professor at a local university. You have always relied on objective final examinations because you feel they are much fairer and give a better picture of your students' performance. You have given the same objective final examination for several years and have gathered extensive normative data on the examination enabling effective year to year comparisons of student performance. This makes the objective final examination even more valuable to you.

One of your best students, John Smith, has asked you for a conference. The student is quite brilliant and creative, but sometimes is short on facts in class discussions. You are now in the middle of the semester and have decided to meet with the student, as requested.

The Basketball Dilemma

Professor's Role (Skilled): You, Peter Remske, are a professor at Syracuse University. You are waiting for a conference with a student who has asked for time to discuss a problem with you. You are aware that the student seemed concerned but are not sure what the problem is all about.

You experience a great deal of satisfaction in your work, particularly when your students are highly successful. You attribute this success to your highly organized and systematic approach to presenting the subject matter. Your carefully planned program of homework is particularly challenging and effective in insuring that students gain knowledge and skills rapidly. While there is a lot of work to your program, you are convinced that the long term payoff is worth it. One of your students, Tom Jones, has requested an appointment. Your position is to use your carefully planned program for student preparation that has proven its effectiveness with all students. You decide to do your best to understand the nature of the student's problem.

Your interests in this situation are:

1. To help students learn knowledge and skills.
2. You want to maintain your reputation as a good teacher.
3. You want to maintain your current good relationship with your students.

Student's Role (Unskilled): You are a college student at Syracuse University, Tom Jones, who has earned satisfactory grades in each subject this semester. Your overall grade point average is 2.5 out of 4.0. You are one of the key players for the varsity basketball team for the school. This involvement offers you a great deal of personal satisfaction and fun, and you are strongly committed to it.

Your specific concern is that the professor assigns a significant amount of homework each night. While it is possible to complete the work and play basketball as well, this means very little free time for you to relax. You decide to see the professor and try to convince him that you should not be given homework as long as you can pass the examinations.

The Workload Dilemma

Administrator's Role (Skilled): You are James Kilpatrick, the administrator of the campus chapel counselling service. This program provides help and support to students who are having difficulty or problems. Lately your work has increased to the point that you must increasingly rely on your volunteer staff to carry out routine duties which you formerly executed yourself. These duties are in addition to the contact work the volunteers originally signed up to do. You have attempted to assign these impartially without overloading any one volunteer too heavily.

Sally Peters, one of your more trusted volunteers, seems to be avoiding you lately. She often doesn't contact the people she has agreed to and does not attend meetings regularly. When you happen to see her and speak to her, she doesn't look at your eyes. Her work is piling up and some of the routine tasks that you have depended on her for have not been completed as she has promised. Your position is for Sally to do the work you have assigned. You decide to confront her.

Your interests in this situation are:

1. You wish to have happy volunteers to help you with the work.
2. Get the work done.
3. You need to share all the work of the program equitably.
4. You want to maintain your current good relationship with the volunteers.

Volunteer's Role (Unskilled): You are Sally Peters, a volunteer in the chapel counselling program. Lately the administrator has turned over routine work to you without lessening the contact work that you have agreed to do. The work requires knowledge that is beyond your experience. You know you are taking an inordinate amount of time to accomplish this and your regular assignments are piling up.

You recently began working an additional evening per week. Some weeks you have skipped meetings. You are feeling overwhelmed and incompetent. You are worried about your ability to meet the administrator's demands and you wonder if he's trying to force you to resign.

The "Walkman" Dilemma

Customer's Role (Skilled): You have recently purchased a Sony "Walkman" cassette recorder from a local high fidelity equipment store. You did considerable research on portable cassette recorders so that you would have a quality unit that would not require frequent repair. You were also careful to purchase the unit from a reputable supplier.

The particular unit that you purchased has not worked well since the beginning. You have taken it into the repair shop three times and now you are there for the fourth time requesting that the unit be replaced with another one. The owner of the store has refused to replace it although he continues to be willing to repair the unit. You think you have purchased a lemon and you want to have justice done in this regard. Your position is to get a new "Walkman" that works well.

Your interests in this situation are:

1. You want to have in your possession a Sony "Walkman" that works well and is dependable.
2. You don't want your valuable time wasted in getting this unit continuously repaired.

Store Owner's Role (Unskilled): You have recently sold a Sony "Walkman" to a customer who continually complains about the functioning of the unit. You have examined the unit three times and can't find anything seriously wrong with it. You have fixed it each time she's brought it in and have listened to it personally to make sure it worked well before it left the store. You think the problem has to do with the way she's using it or the rough treatment she's giving it. You know for a fact that she is a jogger and while running the unit gets a lot of rough usage. The woman has asked you for an appointment to discuss this matter and you have agreed to meet with her.

The Dog Dilemma

Neighbor's Role (Skilled): Your next door neighbor has just acquired a Weimaraner puppy. The dog is very gentle and kind but has chosen to use your backyard as his place for making his messes. You are concerned that if you allow this to continue the dog, when very large, will continue to use your space, forcing you to do a lot of extra clean-up. You do not want this to happen.

You spend a great deal of effort keeping your lawn and shrubs in beautiful condition and you are concerned that the dog's habits will destroy your work. Your position is that the dog always be under control according to the law, either on a leash or under your neighbor's supervision. Your neighbor is a very good, long term friend but you decide to confront him on this question.

Your interests in this situation are:

1. You wish to maintain a good relationship with your next door neighbor.
2. You want to insure that the dog does not mess up your back yard.
3. You want to have the puppy treated with kindness and care.

Owner's Role (Unskilled): You are the owner of a new Weimaraner puppy. You have been spending a lot of energy training the puppy and have been feeling very encouraged that the puppy is now going outside to do his messes. You initially accompanied him outside and were able to exercise some control over where he made his messes. Recently he has become so independent that he does not need to be accompanied. You suspect that he's using the neighbor's yard and not yours but are not sure of this and don't really want to ask.

You are aware that your community has a leash law and your dog should not be allowed to roam about the neighborhood without being on a leash. You feel that this restrains the dog's freedom and is unjust. Your neighbor has just called and asked to come over and chat with you. You suspect he is going to bring up the subject of the dog.

The Library Dilemma

Student's Role (Skilled): You are a student at a large university. You have been doing research on a masters thesis and have been encountering a great deal of difficulty at the school library. You have found the reserve desk librarian is most uncooperative in locating books for you.

Yesterday the librarian refused to allow you to use an important book that you need for your paper that is on reserve by a prestigious professor at the university. The professor has instructed the librarian that no one is to take the book out of the library or use it in the library. He is concerned that someone might steal the book and in that way deprive his students of the use of the book when they want it. This is clearly against library policy and you decide to bring this problem to the attention of the head librarian. Your position is to get the book taken off his own private reserve list and let you have it.

Your interests in this situation are:

1. You want to use the book in the library for your research.
2. You wish to maintain your good relationship with the head librarian.
3. You feel strongly that the rules of the library should be enforced.

Head Librarian's Role (Unskilled): You are the head librarian of the university library. You are fully aware of the rules of the university library which allow that books on reserve be examined in the library by anyone who chooses to look at the book. One professor, however, has given your reserve book librarian special instructions for the books he has on reserve. He insists that only his students may examine the books and that no other students be permitted to look at them while they are on reserve. This violates library policy but the professor involved is very prestigious and influential and is Chairman of the University Senate Committee on Libraries. He is also a personal friend of your superior, the Director of the Library. You are concerned that if you go against his wishes you might be in trouble with your superior and he will take out his frustration and anger on the needs of the library.

Several students have complained about this and you feel really in the middle by the policy on one hand and the professor's wishes on the other. A student has asked for an appointment with you and you think she's going to bring up this question of library policy.

Managing Conflicts of Values

A value is a priority that you choose and act on, after considering alternatives, and that contributes to your self-meaning and enhances your life. A value meets the following criteria:

1. It is discerned and evident in your behavior.
2. It involves a person, object, relationship, or process that:
   - is freely chosen
   - is acted upon
   - gives you positive meaning or purpose
   - enhances your growth.
3. It is always prioritized.*

Conflicts of values include disputes involving beliefs or preferences as well as values. In addition, a value often not only enhances your life but the lives of those around you. Empathy, for example, is a value which can be operationalized as you join the reality of another, through reflective listening to another who has a difficult concern or problem. You are choosing to be in a relationship with the other person at that moment. The process usually enriches your life as well as the life of the other and provides you with a sense of meaning.

A belief, as contrasted with a value, is a choice or an assent of the mind to a statement or truth or fact, beyond observation, on the testimony of another. Beliefs can imply certain values if they are acted upon. A miracle, for example, is a matter of belief. A close friend is diagnosed as having contracted cancer, and 30 days later, without treatment, the cancer disappears. You might well believe that a miracle occurred.

A preference is a choice that doesn't, by itself, imply a value. Preferences do not necessarily give self-meaning or enhance life. For example, you might choose to wear loafers instead of tie shoes. Loafers do not necessarily contribute to your self-meaning or enhance your growth, but you choose them anyway—a preference.

Differences in values, beliefs, and preferences—as well as in habits, opinions, and desires—are common in our society. Such differences often get in the way of harmonious relationships and are a classic source of conflict. It is, in fact, not possible to be alive in this world without finding yourself disagreeing

*Based on Brian P. Hall and Benjamin Tonna. *God's Plans for Us* (New York: Paulist Press, 1980), p. 47.

with others on such matters. The problem is not so much the existence of such differences but rather their constructive management, so that the differences do not create barriers to human interaction.

Particularly when conflicts involve values, the opposing parties experience intense feelings and often seek to persuade each other to accept the opposing view or perspective. In managing conflicts of values, however, the goal is not to convince another to accept your view, but to hear and understand the other's view, respect him or her as a person, and accept the reality that another may see things differently than you.

In managing conflicts of values, it is important to remember that values and beliefs are deeply felt, personal, self-identification experiences that are not easily changed. Values are tied to developmental stages and to the ability to engage new skills. They are not changed through forceful argument, logic, or persuasion. In managing conflicts of values the realistic goal must not be to convince another to accept your view, but to hear, understand and consider the other's view, respect him or her as a person, and accept the reality that another may see, hear and feel things differently than you.

Values conflicts are managed by first using the following seven-step conflict reduction process:

1. *Listen to the other's view using reflective listening skills*—When the other expresses a differing opinion, let him or her know you have heard by reflecting the ideas and feelings accurately and to the other's satisfaction. Get rapport and maintain it at all times during the process.

2. *Summarize the other's view to his or her satisfaction*—When the other has finished expressing his or her view or opinion, summarize the other's view to his or her satisfaction.

3. *Invite the other to hear your view*—In a respectful manner, invite the other to hear your view, carefully using reflective listening skills to hear any resistance. You might say: "It is important for me that you hear my perspective. Would you be willing to listen?"

4. *State your view*—Explain your position clearly, succinctly, and nonevangelistically. The goal is to inform, not to pressure the other into changing his or her view or opinion.

5. *Ask the other to summarize your view to your satisfaction*—In a respectful way, indicate to the other the importance of his or her hearing your view and invite the other to summarize it to your satisfaction.

6. *Summarize and gain agreement on similarities and differences*—Summarizing the similarities and differences in position helps both you and the other clearly understand the differences in values. Often the conversation will continue, with both parties exploring the subtleties of difference. You may well want to repeat steps 1 through 5. In completing the conversation, it is useful for you to summarize the similarities and differences in a respectful way, to enhance mutual respect and mutual clarity about each other's views.

7. *Move to problem solving, if appropriate*—Often the conflict can be resolved easily when both parties hear the other's view. Sometimes differences in needs, however, underlie the differences in values. When this occurs, invite the other to problem solve using the seven step problem solving process.

The use of the Values Conflict Reduction process does not ensure that the difference(s) between two individuals will be eliminated. Sometimes the method results in a resolution of the conflict, with both parties accepting a particular view; often the conflicting parties find themselves much closer than initially anticipated; occasionally there is no change in either position. In those instances in which the disagreement itself remains unresolved, the process provides the opportunity for each person to learn the other's position and for you to hear all the feelings involved and share yours as well, thereby helping normalize the level of emotional energy.

When the Values Conflict Reduction process does not result in a resolution of the conflict, the Seven Step Problem Solving Process (figure 38) can often be effectively used to deal with the remaining differences, especially if the conflict involves underlying needs.

Appendix A
Meta-Model

The Meta-Model is "—an explicit set of information gathering tools designed to reconnect a person's language to the experience represented by his or her language."* The Meta-Model (also named by John Grinder as the Precision Model) helps you hear and respond to the form of the other's communication. Listening in terms of the Meta-Model distinctions will allow you to understand what another is saying with accuracy and clarity.

The Meta-Model distinctions, along with the universal modeling process that the distinction violates are indicated in figure 44. They can be grouped into three categories as follows:

- *Gathering information*—getting a full, complete and accurate representation of experience or the content being represented.

- *Challenging the limits of the speaker's model*—identifying the limits of another's model of the world and challenging it to enrich the other's model.

- *Identifying and challenging semantic ill-formedness*—recognizing sentences that are semantically ill-formed to assist the other in changing portions of his or her model of the world in order to acquire increased choice.

	Universal Modeling Process		
Grouping and Distinction	Deletion	Generalization	Distortion
Gathering Information			
Deletion	X		
Comparative	X		
Lack of referential index		X	
Unspecified verbs		X	
Unspecified nouns		X	
Nominalizations			X
Limits of the Speaker's Model			
Universal quantifiers		X	
Modal operators of necessity and possibility		X	
Semantic Ill-Formedness			
Cause and effect			X
Mind reading			X
Lost performative		X	

Figure 44. Meta-model groupings and distinctions with universal modelling process indicated.

*Leslie Cameron Bandler, *They Lived Happily Ever After* (Cupertino: Meta Publications, 1978), page 171.

Generalizations, deletions and distortions are universal human modelling processes which can be successfully challenged using specifying questions and their variations. The questions and variations for each Meta-Model distinction are indicated in figure 45. Each Meta-Model distinction is described in the following material, with examples to illustrate the appropriate use of specifying questions.

Gathering Information

Gathering information is gaining a complete and accurate description of another's experience in communication. The distinctions included in this grouping are deletion, comparative, lack of referential index, unspecified verbs, unspecified nouns, and nominalizations.

Deletion—A deletion is selectively paying attention to certain aspects of experience and ignoring other aspects. The challenge involves using a specifying question to help another recover the missing or deleted material. Typical specifying questions are indicated in figure 45.

Examples:

Someone says	Challenge (Specifying question)	Prediction
"I'm afraid"	"of what?" or "of whom?"	Recovery of deleted material
"I'm depressed"	"about what?"	Recovery of deleted material
"I don't understand"	"understand what?" or	Recovery of deleted material.
	"How specifically don't you understand?"	Uncovery of representational system.

Comparative—A comparative is a word used without a specific antecedent such as better, worse, easier or best, worst, easiest. A comparative is a special form of deletion. The challenge involves using a specifying question to recover the missing antecedent. Typical specifying questions are indicated in figure 45.

Examples:

Someone says	Challenge (Specifying question)	Prediction
"It's better to do this"	"Better than what?" or "Better than what specifically?"	Recovery of the deleted material.
"He's the best man for the job."	"Better than whom specifically?"	Recovery of the deleted material.
"She's the best listener."	"Amongst whom?" or "Between whom specifically?"	Recovery of the deleted material.
"I'm better."	"Better than whom?"	Recovery of the deleted material.

Lack of referential index—A lack of referential index is a special case of generalization that limits another's model of the world by leaving out detail in such a way that the communication is out of perspective or out of proportion. The challenge involves using a specifying question to make clear exactly to what the noun or pronoun used refers. This results in lack of specificity. Typical specifying questions appear in figure 45.

138

Examples:

Someone says	Challenge (Specifying question)	Prediction
"He likes me"	"Who, specifically, likes you?"	Recovery of specific referential index.
"I don't get along with her."	"Who specifically?"	Recovery of specific referential index.
"This is difficult."	"What specifically?" or "What specifically is difficult?"	Recovery of specific referential index.

Unspecified verb—An unspecified verb is a verb used in a sentence that is not clarified. All verbs are to some extent unspecified, for example *touch* is less specified than *kiss*. The challenge involves using a specifying question to uncover the precise meaning of the verb or its complex equivalent. Typical specifying questions are indicated in figure 45. (A complex equivalent is a generalization in a speakers model when he or she makes one part of a sentence equivalent to another part or one portion of an experience equivalent to or equal to another portion of an experience.)

Examples:

Someone says	Challenges (Specifying question)	Prediction
"She supported me."	"How specifically did she support you?"	Uncovery of more clearly defined verb.
"Tom rejected me."	"How specifically did Tom reject you?"	Uncovery of more clearly defined verb.

Unspecified nouns—An unspecified noun is a person, place or thing which is not defined precisely in communication. Nouns are generally not defined absolutely in dictionaries. The exact definition of a noun varies depending on the experience of the person communicating, that is, any one noun might have as many definitions as the people using it. The word *productivity,* for example, could have several meanings (output per man hour, sales dollars per labor dollar, labor efficiency, machine utilization, etc.). The challenge involves using a specifying question to uncover the precise meaning of the noun to the user. Typical specifying questions are indicated in figure 45.

Examples:

Someone says	Challenge (Specifying questions)	Prediction
"I want a new *job.*"	"What job specifically?"	Uncovery of precise meaning of noun.
"People are very interesting."	"Who, specifically, is interesting."	Uncovery of precise meaning of noun.
"That city is terrific."	"What city, specifically, is terrific?"	Uncovery of precise meaning of noun.

Nominalizations—A nominalization is a verb that has been transformed into a noun. As a consequence, an on-going process is transformed into an event. The challenge involves helping the other see that, what he or she considered as final or finished and is beyond conscious control, is in reality a process which can be changed resulting in more choices for the other. Nominalizations can be distinguished from regular nouns by two tests.

The first test is to ask yourself "Can I put the noun in a wheelbarrow?" If the answer is yes, it is a regular noun, like chair, lamp, hammer, or spade. If the answer is no, it is a nominalization like relationship, virtue, divorce, marriage or love. The second test for a nominalization is to check if the noun fits into the form, "an on-going _____." If it fits it is a nominalization.

The challenge involves transforming the noun to a verb form of the noun. With the noun "relationship," for example, the challenge involves turning it into a process or its verb form "to relate," or "to be related" or "relating" and then using a specifying question to uncover the notion of increased choice.

For example, "How specifically would you like *to relate?*" The challenge helps the other move from passivity in an on-going process to choice. Typical specifying questions are indicated in figure 45.

Examples:

Someone says	*Challenge* (Specifying question)	*Prediction*
"My choice is upsetting me."	"How specifically are you choosing that upsets you?"	Uncovery of increased choice
"I don't get any recognition."	"How specifically would you like to be recognized?"	Uncovery of increased choice
"I have hope."	"For what specifically are you hoping?"	Uncovery of increased choice
"I want help."	"How specifically do you want to be helped?"	Uncovery of increased choice

Challenging the Limits of the Speaker's Model

Challenging the limits of another's model of the world is assisting his or her in enriching and expanding his or her model. The distinctions included in this grouping include universal quantifiers and model operators. Both are generalizations.

Universal quantifiers—A universal quantifier is a generalization that distorts perceptions of reality and prevents another from making distinctions. Such generalizations limit another's available choices. Challenging universal quantifiers assists another in finding the exception to his or her generalization that might offer some new insight to a behavioral alternative. Universal quantifiers include such words as all, every, always, each, nothing, no one, any, never, none, everybody, they. These words essentially lie because they ignore exceptions to the rule.

Three possible challenges to universal quantifiers can be effectively challenged using one of three specifying questions (figure 45).

1. Follow the universal quantifier with a question mark, i.e., "all?," "always?," "never?", etc.

2. Exaggerate, i.e., "You *never, ever*—?"

3. Ask for a contradiction, i.e., "Has there ever been a time when . . . ?"

Examples:

Someone says	*Challenge* (Specifying question)	*Prediction*
"I never do anything right."	"Never?" or "You never, ever do anything right, ever?" or "Has there ever been a time when you did something right?"	Uncovery of counter example.

140

"All I ever do is work."	"All?" or "You never, do anything but work?" "Has there ever been a time when you didn't work?"	Uncovery of counter example.
"None of you should do it."	"None?" or "Absolutely none of us in any circumstances?" "Do you know anyone who does it?"	Uncovery of counter example.

Modal operator's of necessity and possibility—A modal operator of necessity implies that another, in his or her assessment of a situation, has no options or alternative behaviors. A modal operator of possibility denotes inability to do what another desires to do. Some examples include:

Modal operators of possibility	*Modal operators of necessity*
Impossible	Have to
Can't	Necessary
Unable	Must
Couldn't	Should
No way	No choice
	Forced to
	Gotta
	Need
	Ought

The use of modal operators limits choice. Challenging modal operators of possibility takes the other beyond the limits of what was previously accepted as possible. Challenging modal operators of necessity allows other to be more aware of alternatives. Modal operators of possibility or necessity can be effectively challenged by one of three specifying questions (figure 45):

1. "What stops you?" (Past)
2. "What would happen if you did?" (Future)
3. "How do you know?"

Examples:

Someone says	*Challenge* (Specifying question)	*Prediction*
"I can't do it."	"What stops you?" or	Uncovery of cause and effect.
	"What would happen if you did?" or	Uncovery of outcomes or consequences.
	"How do you know you can't?"	Uncovery of complex equivalence.
"It's impossible to complete the assignment on time."	"What's preventing you from completing it?"	Uncovery of complex equivalence.
"I have to do all of the work myself."	"What would happen if you didn't?"	Uncovery of consequences.

Identifying and Challenging Semantic Ill-Formedness

Recognizing and challenging semantically ill-formed sentences helps another identify those portions of his or her experience which are distorted in some way. Challenging semantic ill-formedness provides the other with increased choice and often enables him or her to recognize what doesn't make sense and

141

modify the behavior to what might make more sense. The distinctions included in this grouping include cause and effect, mind reading and lost performative.

Cause and effect—A cause and effect statement is a brief statement that indicates that some action on the part of one individual can cause another individual to experience an emotion. Such statements imply a belief on another's part that one event automatically causes another or that "x" necessarily leads to "y" or how "x" causes "y." Challenging the cause and effect statement allows the other to explore and question rather than causal relationship is true. In challenging you can use a specifying question to uncover how the cause and effect happen in the other's model of the world.

Two possible challenges are available for cause and effect statements, as illustrated in the following examples: (figure 45).

- Cause and effect statement   "Your words infuriate me."
- Challenge uncovering complex equivalence   "How, specifically, does what I'm saying infuriate you?"
- Challenge uncovering cause and effect   "Does my saying _____ necessarily lead you to feel furious?"

Examples:

Someone says	Challenge (Specifying question)	Prediction
"When you look at me it makes my day."	"How, specifically, does my looking at you make your day?"	Uncovery of complex equivalence.
"You frustrate me."	"How specifically do I frustrate you?"	Uncovery of complex equivalence.
"Your saying damn bothers me."	"How does my saying damn necessarily lead you to feel bothered."	Uncovery of complex equivalence.

Mind reading—mind reading is the belief on another's part that one individual can know what another individual is thinking or feeling without direct communication. Challenging mind reading helps the other become aware of the assumptions he or she has made in the statement. The specifying question, "How specifically do you know that _____ ?" uncovers the complex equivalence and fosters ownership of the statement. (figure 45)

Examples:

Someone says	Challenge (Specifying question)	Prediction
"I know you are angry with me."	"How, specifically, do you know that I'm angry with you."	Uncovery of complex equivalence.
"I know just how you feel."	"How, specifically, do you know how I feel?"	Uncovery of complex equivalence.
"You think I'm stupid, don't you?"	"How specifically do I think you're stupid?"	Uncovery of complex equivalence.

Lost performative—a lost performative is a generalization about the world rather than a statement of another owning his or her own experience. In lost performatives the other is often stating his or her opinion as a fact. Cue words in lost performatives include good, bad, crazy, right, wrong, etc. Lost performatives can be effectively challenged using the specifying questions: "For whom?", "According to whom?", or "Who says?".

Examples:

Someone says	Challenge (Specifying question)	Prediction
"It's wrong to take drugs."	"According to whom?"	Recovery of source of opinion.
"That's a sick thing to do!"	"Sick, for whom specifically?"	Recovery of source of opinion.
"It's wrong to argue with your Mom."	"Who says?"	Recovery of source of opinion.

Presupposition—A presupposition is an unstated assumption contained in communication. For example, Carol says, "I'm excited that Jim is turning out to be as productive as his grandfather." The assumption and presupposition is that the grandfather is productive.

To test whether or not you are having a presupposition you can turn the main process word in the sentence into a negative and create a new sentence:

"I'm *not* excited that Jim is turning out to be as productive as his grandfather."

The presupposition is what must be true for both sentences, in this case "grandfather is productive."

Once the presupposition is identified, an appropriate specifying question can be used to challenge the presupposition, for example: "How specifically is grandfather productive?"

Order of challenge—in encountering Meta-Model violations, the following order of challenge is recommended by John Grinder.

1. Presuppositions
2. Deletions, referential indices
3. Universal quantifiers, cause-effect, modal operators, lost performatives, mind reading.

Grouping and Distinction	Purpose of Challenge	Possible Challenges (Specifying Questions)
Gathering Information		
Deletion	Recover deleted material	1. "About whom?" "of whom?" 2. "About what?" "of what?" 3. "How specifically?"
Comparative	Recover deleted material	1. "__ then whom specifically?" 2. "__ then what specifically? 3. "Amongst whom?
Lack of referential index	Recover specific referential index	1. "Who specifically?" 2. "What specifically?"
Unspecified verb	Uncover more clearly defined verb	1. "How, specifically?"
Unspecified noun	Uncover precise meaning of a noun	1. "Who specifically?" 2. "What specifically?"
Nominalization	Move from passivity to choice	1. "How, specifically? 2. "For what, specifically, are you ____ ing?"
Challenging the Limits of the Speakers Model		
Universal quantifier	Uncover counter example	1. Add question mark (?) 2. Exaggerate 3. Ask for a contradiction
Modal operators of possibility and necessity	Uncover cause and effect, consequences or outcomes, or complex equivalent	"What stops you?" "What would happen if you did?" "How do you know?"
Identifying and Challenging Semantic Ill-Formedness		
Cause and effect	Uncover complex equivalent Uncover cause and effect	"How specifically . . . ?" "Does my saying ____ necessarily lead you to feel ____?"
Mind Reading	Recover complex equivalent	"How specifically do you know that . . . ?"
Lost performative	Recover source of opinion Recover source of opinion Recover source of opinion	"According to whom?" "Who says?" "For whom?"

Figure 45. Meta-model questions and variations.

Appendix B
Feeling Words

All too often, in attempting to describe our own feelings or reflect the feelings of another, we settle—through habit or lack of a varied vocabulary of feeling words—for a general, all-purpose term. We describe ourselves as "happy," for instance, when our emotion of the moment might more exactly be characterized as "euphoric." We tentatively reflect to another that we perceive he or she is feeling "sad," when the other may, in fact, be feeling "uncared-for" or "weary."

When we fail to choose a word that captures our own or the other's feelings precisely, however, we also fail to communicate as fully as we might—we miss the opportunity to enhance our understanding of each other and thereby increase the distance between ourselves and the other.

The following listing constitutes a "mini-thesaurus" of "positive" and "negative" feeling words. Both individual feeling words and groups of related words are presented, in alphabetical order, with many of the entries cross-referenced to still other related word groups. While its coverage is not exhaustive, and the word groups must at times be somewhat arbitrary, this listing should nonetheless provide a good starting place for increasing your personal repertoire of feeling words with which you can capture and express your own emotions or those of another.

Positive Feeling Words

Accepted (*see also:* **loved, trusted**)

Accepting, open, receptive, responsive, sociable, trusting

Adequate (*see also:* **confident**)

Admired, esteemed, important, looked up to, respected, well-regarded

Adored (*see also:* **loved**)

Adventurous, daring

Affectionate (*see also:* **loving**)

Affirmed (*see also:* **loved, supported, trusted**)

Alert (*see also:* **alive, perceptive**)

Alive, alert, animated, buoyant, bubbly, effervescent, energetic, invigorated, lively, refreshed, renewed, revitalized, turned-on, vibrant, vivacious, wide awake (*see also:* **excited**)

Amazed (*see also:* **surprised**)

Amused (*see also:* **delighted**)

Animated (*see also:* **alive, excited**)

Anxious (*see also:* **excited**)

Appealing

Appreciated (*see also:* **loved, trusted**)

Appreciative, grateful, thankful

Approved (*see also:* **loved, trusted**)

Ardent (*see also:* **loving**)

Astonished (*see also:* **surprised**)

At ease (*see also:* **calm**)

At peace (*see also:* **calm, comfortable**)

Attentive (*see also:* **perceptive**)

Attractive, beautiful, handsome, lovely

Aware (*see also:* **perceptive**)

Awed (*see also:* **inspired, surprised**)

Beautiful (*see also:* **attractive**)

Benevolent, generous, kindly

Bewitched (*see also:* **delighted**)

Brave, courageous, valiant

Brilliant (*see also:* **talented**)

Bubbly (*see also:* **alive**)

Buoyant (*see also:* **alive**)

Calm, at ease, at peace, comfortable, composed, peaceful, quiet, relaxed, safe, satisfied, serene, sustained, tranquil, untroubled

Capable (*see also:* **confident**)

Captivated (*see also:* **delighted**)

Cared for (*see also:* **loved**)

Caring (*see also:* **loving, sympathetic, thoughtful**)

Certain (*see also:* **positive**)

Cheerful (*see also:* **happy**)

Childlike, innocent (*see also:* **free**)

Comfortable, at peace, cozy, peaceful, warm (*see also:* **calm**)

Comforted, consoled

Competent (*see also:* **confident**)

Composed (*see also:* **calm**)

Concerned (*see also:* **loving, sympathetic, thoughtful**)

Confident, adequate, capable, competent

Considerate (*see also:* **thoughtful**)

Considered (*see also:* **loved**)

Consoled, comforted

Contented (*see also:* **happy**)

Cordial, friendly, hospitable, warm, welcomed

Courageous (*see also:* **brave**)

Cozy (*see also:* **comfortable**)

Creative

Curious, fascinated, inquisitive

Daring, adventurous

Delighted, amused, bewitched, captivated, enchanted (*see also:* **excited, happy**)

Delirious (*see also:* **happy**)

Deserving (*see also:* **worthy**)

Determined, purposeful, tenacious

Eager, zealous (*see also:* **excited**)

Ecstatic (*see also:* **excited, happy**)

Effervescent (*see also:* **alive**)

Elated (*see also:* **excited**)

Empathic (*see also:* **sympathetic**)

Enamored (*see also:* **loving**)

Enchanted (*see also:* **delighted, happy**)

Encouraged (*see also:* **supported**)

Energetic (*see also:* **alive**)

Enlightened, enriched (*see also:* **inspired**)

Enriched (*see also:* **enlightened**)

Enthusiastic (*see also:* **excited, optimistic**)

Entranced (*see also:* **happy**)

Esteemed (*see also:* **admired**)

Euphoric (*see also:* **happy**)

Excited, animated, anxious, delighted, eager, ecstatic, elated, enthusiastic, stimulated, thrilled, turned-on (*see also:* **alive, delighted, happy**)

Expectant (*see also:* **optimistic**)

Expressive (*see also:* **free**)

Fascinated (*see also:* **curious, interested**)

Flabbergasted (*see also:* **surprised**)

Fortunate, lucky

Free, childlike, expressive, independent, outgoing, unencumbered

Friendly (*see also:* **cordial**)

Fulfilled (*see also:* **enlightened, inspired, satisfied**)

Gay (*see also:* **happy**)

Generous (*see also:* **benevolent**)

Gentle (*see also:* **sensitive**)

Giddy (*see also:* **happy**)

Glad (*see also:* **happy**)

Glamorous

Good

Graceful, poised

Gracious

Grateful (*see also:* **appreciative**)

Gratified (*see also:* **satisfied**)

Great

Gregarious (*see also:* **optimistic**)

Handsome (*see also:* **attractive**)

Happy, cheerful, contented, delighted, delirious, ecstatic, enchanted, entranced, euphoric, gay, giddy, glad, intoxicated, jolly, joyful, jubilant, overjoyed, overpowered, pleased, thrilled, transported (*see also:* **excited**)

Healthy, well

Hopeful (*see also:* **optimistic**)

Hospitable (*see also:* **cordial**)

Important (*see also:* **admired**)

Impressed (*see also:* **inspired**)

Included (*see also:* **loved**)

Independent (*see also:* **free**)

In earnest, sincere

Infatuated (*see also:* **loving**)

Innocent, childlike

Inquisitive (*see also:* **curious**)

Inspired, awed, enlightened, fulfilled, impressed, transported, uplifted

Intelligent (*see also:* **talented**)

Interested, fascinated, stimulated

Intoxicated (*see also:* **happy**)

Invigorated (*see also:* **alive**)

Jolly (*see also:* **happy**)

Joyful (*see also:* **happy**)

Jubilant (*see also:* **happy**)

Kindly (*see also:* **benevolent**)

Liked

Lively (*see also:* **alive**)

Looked up to (*see also:* **admired**)

Loved, accepted, adored, affirmed, approved, cared for, considered, included, needed, popular, protected, safe, secure, supported, understood, wanted (*see also:* **trusted**)

Lovely (*see also:* **attractive**)

Loving, affectionate, ardent, caring, concerned, enamored, infatuated, passionate

Lucky, fortunate

Masterful

Needed (*see also:* **loved**)

Open, trusting (*see also:* **accepting**)

Optimistic, enthusiastic, expectant, gregarious, hopeful, outgoing

Outgoing (*see also:* **free, optimistic**)

Overjoyed (*see also:* **happy**)

Overpowered (*see also:* **happy**)

Passionate (*see also:* **loving**)

Patient

Peaceful (*see also:* **calm, comfortable**)

Pensive, thoughtful

Perceptive, alert, attentive, aware

Pitying (*see also:* **sympathetic**)

Pleased (*see also:* **happy, satisfied**)

Poised, graceful (*see also:* **talented**)

Popular (*see also:* **loved**)

Positive, certain, right, sure

Powerful, strong

Productive (*see also:* **talented**)

Prosperous (*see also:* **rich**)

Protected (*see also:* **loved**)

Protective

Proud (*see also:* **satisfied**)

Purposeful (*see also:* **determined, talented**)

Quiet (*see also:* **calm**)

Receptive (*see also:* **accepting**)

Refreshed (*see also:* **alive**)

Relaxed (*see also:* **calm**)

Relieved

Renewed (*see also:* **alive**)

Respected (*see also:* **admired**)

Responsive (*see also:* **accepting**)

Revitalized (*see also:* **alive**)

Rich, prosperous, successful

Right (*see also:* **positive**)

Romantic, sentimental, thoughtful

Safe (*see also:* **calm, loved**)

Satisfied, fulfilled, gratified, pleased, proud, triumphant (*see also:* **calm**)

Secure (*see also:* **loved**)

Seductive

Sensitive, gentle, tender

Sentimental (*see also:* **romantic**)

Serene (*see also:* **calm**)

Sincere, in earnest

Smart (*see also:* **talented**)

Sociable (*see also:* **accepting**)

Spiritual

Stimulated (*see also:* **excited, interested**)

Strong, powerful

Successful (*see also:* **rich, talented**)

Supported, affirmed, encouraged, sustained (*see also:* **loved**)

Sure (*see also:* **positive**)

Surprised, amazed, astonished, awed, flabbergasted

Sustained (*see also:* **calm, supported**)

Sympathetic, caring, concerned, empathic, pitying, tactful

Tactful (*see also:* **sympathetic**)

Talented, brilliant, gifted, intelligent, poised, productive, purposeful, smart, successful

Tenacious (*see also:* **determined**)

Tender (*see also:* **sensitive**)

Thankful (*see also:* **appreciative**)

Thoughtful, caring, concerned, considerate, pensive (*see also:* **romantic**)

Thrilled (*see also:* **excited, happy**)

Tranquil (*see also:* **calm**)

Transported (*see also:* **happy, inspired**)

Triumphant, victorious (*see also:* **satisfied**)

Trusted, accepted, affirmed, appreciated, approved (*see also:* **loved**)

Trusting (*see also:* **accepting**)

Turned-on (*see also:* **alive, excited**)

Understood (*see also:* **loved**)

Unencumbered (*see also:* **free**)

Untroubled (*see also:* **calm**)

Uplifted (*see also:* **inspired**)

Valiant (*see also:* **brave**)

Vibrant (*see also:* **alive**)

Victorious, triumphant

Virile

Vivacious (*see also:* **alive**)

Wanted (*see also:* **loved, worthy**)

Warm (*see also:* **comfortable, cordial**)

Welcomed (*see also:* **cordial**)

Well, healthy

Well-regarded (*see also:* **admired**)

Wide awake (*see also:* **alive**)

Worthy, deserving, desired, wanted

Zealous, eager

Negative Feeling Words

Abandoned (*see also:* **alone, unloved**)

Afraid (*see also:* **frightened**)

Agitated (*see also:* **upset, wild**)

Alarmed (*see also:* **frightened, upset**)

Alienated, estranged, withdrawn (*see also:* **cold, unloved**)

Alone, abandoned, apart, avoided, isolated, left-out, lonely, neglected, unpopular, unwelcome (*see also:* **unloved**)

Amazed (*see also:* **shocked**)

Angry, fuming, furious, hateful, indignant, infuriated, livid, mad, provoked, resentful, seething (*see also:* **hostile, upset**)

Annoyed (*see also:* **bothered, upset**)

Antagonistic (*see also:* **hostile**)

Anxious (*see also:* **bothered, restless, uncomfortable**)

Apart (*see also:* **alone, cold, unloved**)

Apathetic, lethargic, listless (*see also:* **defeated, disinterested**)

Appalled (*see also:* **disgusted, shocked**)

Appeased (*see also:* **burdensome, frustrated**)

Apprehensive (*see also:* **frightened, upset**)

Arrogant (*see also:* **disdainful**)

Ashamed (*see also:* **embarrassed**)

At a loss (*see also:* **shocked, uncomfortable**)

Avoided (*see also:* **alone, burdensome, unloved**)

Bad, inferior, naughty, worthless

Bashful, inhibited, insecure, self-conscious, shy, timid (*see also:* **embarrassed, inadequate**)

Belittled (*see also:* **put-down**)

Bewildered (*see also:* **confused**)

Bitter (*see also:* **hostile**)

Bored (*see also:* **disinterested**)

Bothered, annoyed, anxious, discontented, distressed, edgy, fussed, ill at ease, pestered, put-out, troubled, worried (*see also:* **upset**)

Burdensome, avoided, appeased, dependent, disliked, in the way, put up with, tolerated

Caged (*see also:* **frustrated**)

Callous (*see also:* **cold, unfeeling**)

Cautious (*see also:* **frightened**)

Censored (*see also:* **frustrated, put-down**)

Cold, apart, callous, indifferent, lukewarm, stiff (*see also:* **alienated, dead, unfeeling**)

Confined (*see also:* **frustrated**)

Confused, bewildered, mixed-up, perplexed, unsure

Conquered (*see also:* **defeated**)

Contemptuous (*see also:* **disgusted, hostile**)

Controlled (*see also:* **frustrated, manipulated**)

Cornered (*see also:* **frustrated**)

Cynical

Dead, dull, numb (*see also:* **cold, shocked, unfeeling**)

Defeated, apathetic, conquered, depressed, discouraged, exhausted, failed, forlorn, helpless, hopeless, impotent, overpowered, resigned, submissive, weak

Degraded (*see also:* **put down**)

Dejected (*see also:* **hurt, sad**)

Dependent (*see also:* **burdensome, inadequate**)

Depressed (*see also:* **defeated, sad, susceptible**)

Desperate

Despised (*see also:* **unloved**)

Detested (*see also:* **unloved**)

Disappointed, let down (*see also:* **sad**)

Disconsolate (*see also:* **sad**)

Discontented (*see also:* **bothered, uncomfortable**)

Discouraged (*see also:* **defeated, frustrated**)

Disdainful, arrogant, superior (*see also:* **disgusted, hostile**)

Disgusted, appalled, contemptuous, fed-up, repelled, repulsed, sick (*see also:* **disdainful**)

Disinterested, bored, indifferent, listless, unconcerned (*see also:* **apathetic**)

Disliked (*see also:* **burdensome, put-down, unloved**)

Dismayed (*see also:* **shocked, upset**)

Dissatisfied

Distressed (*see also:* **bothered, uncomfortable, upset**)

Disturbed (*see also:* **upset**)

Dreadful

Dull (*see also:* **dead, unfeeling**)

Edgy (*see also:* **bothered, restless, uncomfortable, upset**)

Embarassed, ashamed, humiliated, mortified, shamed (*see also:* **bashful**)

Emotional (*see also:* **upset**)

Envious (*see also:* **jealous**)

Estranged (*see also:* **alienated, unloved**)

Exhausted (*see also:* **defeated, tired**)

Exploitative (*see also:* **meddlesome**)

Exploited (*see also:* **manipulated**)

Failed (*see also:* **defeated**)

Fatigued (*see also:* **tired**)

Fearful (*see also:* **frightened**)

Fed-up (*see also:* **disgusted**)

Fidgety (*see also:* **uncomfortable**)

Fighting (*see also:* **resistant**)

Forlorn (*see also:* **defeated, hurt, sad, unloved**)

Frantic (*see also:* **frightened, upset, wild**)

Frightened, afraid, alarmed, apprehensive, cautious, fearful, frantic, horrified, panicky, scared, terrified

Frozen (*see also:* **shocked**)

Frustrated, appeased, caged, censored, confined, controlled, cornered, discouraged, held back, restrained, stifled, trapped, thwarted

Fuming (*see also:* **angry**)

Furious (*see also:* **angry**)

Fussed (*see also:* **bothered, upset**)

Gloomy, moody, sullen (*see also:* **sad**)

Grief-stricken (*see also:* **sad**)

Guilty

Hated (*see also:* **unloved**)

Hateful (*see also:* **angry, unloved**)

Headstrong (*see also:* **wild**)

Held back (*see also:* **frustrated, put-down**)

Helpless (*see also:* **defeated, inadequate, susceptible**)

Hopeless (*see also:* **defeated, sad**)

Horrified (*see also:* **frightened**)

Hostile, antagonistic, bitter, contemptuous, vengeful (*see also:* **angry, disdainful**)

Humiliated (*see also:* **embarrassed**)

Hurt, dejected, forlorn, injured, pained

Hysterical (*see also:* **upset, wild**)

Ignored (*see also:* **unloved**)

Ill at ease (*see also:* **bothered, uncomfortable**)

Immobilized (*see also:* **shocked**)

Impatient (*see also:* **uncomfortable**)

Impetuous, impulsive

Imposed upon (*see also:* **manipulated**)

Impotent (*see also:* **defeated, inadequate, susceptible**)

Impulsive, impetuous

Inadequate, dependent, helpless, impotent, incapable, ineffectual, inferior, insecure, unimportant, unworthy, useless, worthless (*see also:* **bashful**)

Incapable (*see also:* **inadequate**)

Indifferent (*see also:* **cold, disinterested**)

Indignant (*see also:* **angry, shocked, upset**)

Ineffectual (*see also:* **inadequate**)

Inferior (*see also:* **bad, inadequate, put-down**)

Infuriated (*see also:* **angry**)

Inhibited (*see also:* **bashful**)

Injured (*see also:* **hurt**)

Insecure (*see also:* **bashful, inadequate**)

In the way (*see also:* **burdensome**)

Irritated (*see also:* **upset**)

Isolated (*see also:* **alone, unloved**)

Jealous, envious, suspicious

Left out (*see also:* **alone, unloved**)

Let down, disappointed (*see also:* **sad**)

Lethargic (*see also:* **apathetic**)

Listless (*see also:* **apathetic, disinterested**)

Livid (*see also:* **angry**)

Lonely (*see also:* **alone**)

Lukewarm (*see also:* **cold**)

Mad (*see also:* **angry**)

Managed (*see also:* **manipulated**)

Maneuvered (*see also:* **manipulated**)

Manipulated, controlled, exploited, imposed upon, managed, maneuvered, placated, used

Manipulating (*see also:* **meddlesome**)

Meddlesome, exploitative, manipulating

Melancholy (*see also:* **sad**)

Miserable (*see also:* **sad**)

Mixed-up (*see also:* **confused**)

Moody (*see also:* **gloomy, sad**)

Morose (*see also:* **sad**)

Mortified (*see also:* **embarrassed**)

Naughty (*see also:* **bad**)

Negative (*see also:* **resistant**)

Neglected (*see also:* **alone, unloved**)

Nervous (*see also:* **restless, uncomfortable**)

Numb (*see also:* **dead, shocked**)

Obtuse (*see also:* **resistant**)

Out of control (*see also:* **wild**)

Overpowered (*see also:* **defeated**)

Overworked (*see also:* **pressured**)

Pained (*see also:* **hurt**)

Panicky (*see also:* **frightened, wild**)

Paralyzed (*see also:* **shocked**)

Passive

Perplexed (*see also:* **confused**)

Perturbed (*see also:* **upset**)

Pessimistic (*see also:* **resistant**)

Pestered (*see also:* **bothered**)

Picked on (*see also:* **pressured**)

Placated (*see also:* **manipulated**)

Powerless (*see also:* **susceptible**)

Pressured, overworked, picked on, put upon

Provoked (*see also:* **angry**)

Put-down, belittled, censored, degraded, disliked, held back, inferior, repressed, stifled, subdued

Put up with (*see also:* **burdensome**)

Regretful (*see also:* **sad**)

149

Rejected (*see also:* **unloved**)

Reluctant (*see also:* **resistant**)

Repelled (*see also:* **disgusted**)

Repressed (*see also:* **put-down**)

Repulsed (*see also:* **disgusted**)

Resentful (*see also:* **angry, resistant**)

Resigned (*see also:* **defeated**)

Resistant, fighting, negative, obtuse, pessimistic, reluctant, resentful, stubborn, subversive, unreasonable

Restless, anxious, edgy, nervous, tense (*see also:* **uncomfortable, upset**)

Restrained (*see also:* **frustrated**)

Sad, dejected, depressed, disappointed, disconsolate, forlorn, grief-stricken, hopeless, let-down, melancholy, miserable, morose, regretful, torn-up, unhappy (*see also:* **gloomy**)

Scared (*see also:* **frightened**)

Seething (*see also:* **angry**)

Self-conscious (*see also:* **bashful**)

Sensitive, touchy

Shaken (*see also:* **shocked, upset**)

Shamed (*see also:* **embarrassed**)

Shocked, amazed, appalled, at a loss, dead, dismayed, frozen, immobilized, indignant, numb, paralyzed, shaken, stunned

Shy (*see also:* **bashful**)

Sick (*see also:* **disgusted**)

Stiff (*see also:* **cold, unfeeling**)

Stifled (*see also:* **frustrated, put-down**)

Stubborn (*see also:* **resistant**)

Stunned (*see also:* **shocked**)

Subdued (*see also:* **put-down**)

Submissive (*see also:* **defeated**)

Subversive (*see also:* **resistant**)

Sullen (*see also:* **gloomy, sad**)

Superior (*see also:* **disdainful**)

Susceptible, depressed, helpless, impotent, powerless, threatened, vulnerable, weak

Suspicious (*see also:* **jealous**)

Tense (*see also:* **restless, uncomfortable**)

Terrified (*see also:* **frightened**)

Threatened (*see also:* **susceptible**)

Thwarted (*see also:* **frustrated**)

Timid (*see also:* **bashful**)

Tired, exhausted, fatigued, weary, worn-out

Tolerated (*see also:* **burdensome**)

Tormented, tortured

Torn-up (*see also:* **sad**)

Tortured, tormented

Touchy, sensitive

Trapped (*see also:* **frustrated**)

Troubled (*see also:* **bothered, upset**)

Unacceptable (*see also:* **unloved**)

Unbalanced (*see also:* **upset**)

Uncared-for (*see also:* **unloved**)

Uncaring (*see also:* **unfeeling**)

Uncomfortable, anxious, at a loss, discontented, distressed, edgy, fidgety, ill at ease, impatient, nervous, tense, uneasy (*see also:* **restless**)

Unconcerned (*see also:* **disinterested**)

Undemonstrative (*see also:* **unfeeling**)

Uneasy (*see also:* **uncomfortable**)

Unfeeling, callous, dull, stiff, uncaring, undemonstrative, unloving (*see also:* **cold, dead**)

Unimportant (*see also:* **inadequate**)

Unloved, abandoned, apart, avoided, despised, detested, disliked, forlorn, hated, hateful, ignored, isolated, left out, neglected, rejected, unacceptable, uncared-for, unpopular, unwanted, unwelcome, useless (*see also:* **alienated, alone**)

Unloving (*see also:* **unfeeling**)

Unpopular (*see also:* **alone, unloved**)

Unreasonable (*see also:* **resistant**)

Unsure (*see also:* **confused**)

Unwanted (*see also:* **unloved**)

Unwelcome (*see also:* **alone, unloved**)

Unworthy (*see also:* **inadequate**)

Upset, agitated, alarmed, annoyed, apprehensive, bothered, dismayed, distressed, disturbed, edgy, emotional, frantic, fussed, hysterical, indignant, irritated, perturbed, shaken, troubled, unbalanced, uptight, worried (*see also:* **angry, restless, wild**)

Uptight (*see also:* **upset**)

Used (*see also:* **manipulated**)

Useless (*see also:* **inadequate, unloved**)

Vengeful (*see also:* **hostile**)

Vulnerable (*see also:* **susceptible**)

Weak (*see also:* **defeated, susceptible**)

Weary (*see also:* **tired**)

Wild, agitated, frantic, headstrong, hysterical, out of control, panicky (*see also:* **upset**)

Withdrawn (*see also:* **alienated**)

Worn-out (*see also:* **tired**)

Worried (*see also:* **bothered, upset**)

Worthless (*see also:* **bad, inadequate**)

Appendix C
Human Needs

Abraham Maslow theorized that needs are the primary influencers on an individual's behavior. When a particular need emerges, it determines your behavior in terms of motivation and action taken. Thus motivated behavior is the result of the tension—either pleasant or unpleasant—experienced when a need presents itself. The goal of the behavior is the reduction of this tension or discomfort, and the behavior, itself, will be appropriate for facilitating the satisfaction of the need. Only unsatisfied needs are prime sources of motivation.

Understanding behaviors and their goals involves gaining insight into presently unsatisfied needs. Maslow developed a method for gaining insight by providing categories of needs in a hierarchical structure. He placed all human needs, from primitive or immature (in terms of the behaviors they foster) to civilized or mature needs, into five need systems. He believed that there is a natural process whereby individuals fulfill needs in ascending order from most immature to most mature. This progression through the need hierarchy is viewed as climbing a ladder where you must experience secure footing on the first rung in order to move up to the next higher level. The awareness of the need to climb further up the ladder is a function of having fulfilled the felt need. Only the satisfactory fulfillment of this need will allow you to deal with the next higher level. The inability to fulfill a lower-order need or difficulty in fulfilling a lower-order need may result in your "locking in" on immature behavior patterns or may produce a tendency to return to immature behaviors under stress any time you feel a lower-order need not fulfilled to your satisfaction. The individual may also revert to behaviors which fulfilled lower-order needs when the satisfaction of higher needs are temporarily blocked. That is not to say that any need is ever completely satisfied; rather, Maslow indicates that there must be at least partial fulfillment before you can become aware of the tensions manifested by a higher-order need and have the freedom to pursue its fulfillment.

The Maslow Need Hierarchy is presented in figure 46. The basic level represents needs which reflect physiological and survival goals. At this level are such factors as shelter, clothing, food, sex, and other necessities. In a culture such as ours, where these basic needs are usually met, there is not likely to be any need tension concerning the fulfillment of basic needs. However, individuals adapt this basic level to include such needs as avoidance of physical discomfort, pleasant working environment, or more money for providing creature comforts. This adaptation often causes tension at the basic need level.

The second level of the hierarchy consists of safety needs. When the individual has at least partially fulfilled the basic needs, he or she will experience the tensions relating to needs of security; orderliness, protective rules, and general risk avoidance. These needs are often satisfied by an adequate salary, insurance policies, a good burglar alarm system for a home, a security guard for an apartment building, etc.

When safety needs have been met, the individual will become less preoccupied with self and will endeavor to form interpersonal relationships. The relative success of this need for belonging will result in your feeling accepted and appreciated by others. Thus, the third level needs concern family ties, friendship and group membership.

MASLOW'S NEEDS HIERARCHY

Level	General Context	Work Context
I	The basic needs of the physical organism for nourishment, protection from the elements, warmth.	The needs from the work environment for basic warmth and comfort. More importantly, you expect to be paid enough to ensure these basic needs in your private life.
II	The needs to be assured of the continuation of safety in the environment and social setting into the proximate future. Norms and rules.	Job security, to ensure that basic needs will be met in the future, as well as a physically safe work environment and freedom from threat to you.
III	The needs to be affirmed and valued by your community of peers and by those with whom you are in contact. Stroking, comforting when hurt, caring are important. Affectional needs.	The needs to have your judgment and insight respected; to be listened to and taken seriously. You need to know that you are liked, and have a community on which you can count for support.
IV	The needs to know yourself to be a contributing member of society, carrying your share of the load. A need to develop skills common to your reference group and also unique to yourself, and be valued and esteemed for them.	The needs to know that you have contributed something of value to your organization, and have that corroborated by others as well as feel satisfied with the job you are able to do.
V	The needs to extend yourself into new stages of growth unique to yourself; employ your creativity and develop new patterns that please you.	The need to develop new constructs, hypotheses, fantasies and connections and explore, test and share them with others.

Figure 46. Maslow's needs hierarchy.

When an individual feels secure in his or her relationships with others, he or she will probably seek to gain special status within the group. This tension will be associated with ambition and a desire to excel. These ego-status needs will motivate you to seek out opportunities to display your competence in an effort to gain social and professional rewards.

Because ego-status fulfillment is greatly dependent upon the ability of others to respond appropriately to the individual's efforts to perform in a superior way, they are the most difficult to fulfill satisfactorily. However, if you have gained satisfaction on level four, you may be able to move up to level five—self actualization. At this level, you are concerned with personal growth and may fulfill this need by challenging yourself to become more creative, demanding greater self achievement, and, in general, directing yourself to measure up to your own criteria of personal success. Self-actualizing behaviors must include risk taking, seeking autonomy, and developing freedom to act.

Figure 46 describes the needs in Maslow's hierarchy in both a general and a work context.

Needs as a Key to Understanding Self and Others

The list that follows is an elaboration of Maslow's hierarchy of human needs. It may help bring clarity to your needs and even suggest words for needs that you vaguely feel, but have not been able to identify. The list may also aid you in understanding others and suggest how to help them: identify what others need and, if appropriate, help them get it. Thus a needs list is useful for those helping others grow.

The items on this list are referred to as "needs" because people tend to experience them as requirements for fulfillment. When circumstances allow others to get these things, they tend to feel comfortably alive. When circumstances prevent others from getting them, they tend to feel frustrated, incomplete, dissatisfied, and unhealthy. It is in that sense that people "need" them. Individuals need the items on the list differently, and in differing amounts. The key question is which needs are important for a particular person at a particular time.

The "Needs List" below is not meant to be exhaustive, and its organization is in no way absolute. It is just one list of needs that human beings in our culture often experience and that might prove useful in viewing both yourself and others.

NEEDS LIST

	Samples of feelings that arise when need is:	
	Satisfied	*Unsatisfied*
Physical Needs		
Survival conditions—food, oxygen, viable temperature range, etc.	Not physically pressured	Physically tense
Remedies—drugs, surgery, eye glasses, physical therapy, rest when weak, etc.	At ease	Distress
Physical comforts—tasty food, comfortable temperature, soft chairs, etc.	Comfortable	Discomfort
Safety Needs		
Security—certainty that other needs will be met, rhythm in life, support when weak, orderliness, having a place in society, freedom from terror, etc.	Secure	Fearful
Freedom from excessive pressure—having within tolerable limits such things as change, problems, conflict, disorganization, stimulation, work pressures; time to be alone, to think, to relax, etc.	Relaxed, on top of things	Pressured
Affection Needs		
Affection—feelings of warmth and acceptance from others, being treated with affection, giving and receiving favors, being liked, etc.	Warm	Detached (from others)
Belonging—being with others, socializing, being included, sharing, having friends and family, chatting, teamwork, etc.	Accepted	Lonelypet

NEEDS LIST—*Continued*

Samples of feelings that arise when need is:

	Satisfied	Unsatisfied
Love and intimacy—deep interpersonal understanding and feeling, devotion, nonjudgmental caring acceptance, etc.	Deep human attachment	Alone

Action Needs

	Satisfied	Unsatisfied
Activity—doing things, solving problems, moving about, thinking, working, satisfying curiosity, exercise, etc.	Alive, energetic	Lethargic, dull lazy
Influence—making a difference, being listened to, having an effect upon things or people, etc.	Significant	Ineffective
Power—being in control, acting willfully, asserting oneself strongly, being a leader, etc.	Powerful	Blocked
Expression—expressing your emotions and thoughts, producing art works, being playful and gay, sharing problems, etc.	Released, open	Stifled

Achievement Needs

	Satisfied	Unsatisfied
Accomplishment—feeling successful and capable, making progress, achieving a goal, resisting distracting impulses, making wise decisions, etc.	Productive, competent	Incapable
Recognition—respect from others; being praised, admired as competent; approval for worthy behavior, considered as an important person, being known by others, etc.	Respected, noticed	Unappreciated, unimportant

Growth Needs

	Satisfied	Unsatisfied
Stimulation—excitement; stimulation of sight, sound, touch, smell, traveling, variety, new ideas; change etc.	Stimulated	Bored
Development—becoming better, moving to more complex levels of being, advancing to new life processes, growing, moving through developmental levels, etc.	Mature, enriched, growing	Static, defeated, listless

	Samples of feelings that arise when need is:	
	Satisfied	*Unsatisfied*

Freedom Needs

<u>Space for Autonomy</u>—room to be yourself, self-direction, private territory, space for exploration, making your own choices, resisting the control of others, etc.

	Satisfied	*Unsatisfied*
Space for Autonomy	Free	Controlled

<u>Being Constructive and Creative</u>— contributing, building, creating new forms, imagining, being idealistic, discovering better ways, helping, etc.

	Satisfied	*Unsatisfied*
Being Constructive and Creative	Proud, worthwhile	Uncreative, unhelpful

<u>Understanding</u>—knowing what is happening, the names for things, how things work, and what is likely to happen in the future; being able to make sense of your perceptions; satisfying curiosity; seeing models that might be emulated, etc.

	Satisfied	*Unsatisfied*
Understanding	Informed, wise	Unaware, naive, stupid

<u>Skills</u>—being able to do things, necessary and pleasurable; developing physical and mental talents; reading, swimming, conversing, managing, etc.

	Satisfied	*Unsatisfied*
Skills	Skillful	Unable, clumsy

Integrating Needs

<u>Time integration</u>—building continuity between the present and both the past and the future, finishing tasks, looking forward to the future, organizing your time, etc.

	Satisfied	*Unsatisfied*
Time integration	Good perspective	Disoriented, inconsistent, aimless

Integrating Needs

<u>Self integration</u>—building harmony among your thoughts, your feelings and your behaviors; coming to terms with your positive and negative impulses; dealing with any gap between your real self and ideal self; self-acceptance, etc.

	Satisfied	*Unsatisfied*
Self integration	Whole, unified, congruent	Conflictful, guilty

Samples of feelings that arise
when need is:

Satisfied	Unsatisfied
Well-adjusted, responsible	Unsettled, selfish, exploited

Self-society integration—unifying the
satisfaction of your own needs with others'
needs; dealing with environmental demands,
accepting your place, getting along in the
world; being a part of a compatible social
unit; etc.

When you see yourself and others in terms of needs, behaviors and frustrations often become more
clear. Understanding needs thus provides a key to identifying what might be lacking in your current life
experience as well as what kinds of actions you might take to enrich your experience. Your current experiences may not be providing and enabling that need to be satisfied.

Appendix D
Values Discernment

Brian Hall in his work on value defines a value as a "priority that I choose and act on that creatively enhances my life and the lives of those around me."* The word value is a nominalization of the verb "to value" which indicates a process that is continuous throughout a person's life. The words assigned to values are names for experience that indicate priorities. What is specifically chosen by an individual is a person, object, process or relationship. The "why" of the choice points to the value. Brian Hall constructed a list of values over a period of several years which appears in figure 47.

Brian Hall postulated that as people mature they pass through four phases of consciousness and that people are able to internalize certain values in specific phases of consciousness. The developmental continuum, "The Four Phases in the Development of Consciousness" and the "Eight Stages in the Development of Values" are shown in figure 48. All 120 values are distributed on a "Value Continuum" in figure 49. Brian Hall suggests that people are born with all 120 values but they experience them in accordance with their specific phase of development (figure 50).

Each person operationalizes a range of values with each particular experience. As you reflect on your experience and identify the values implicit in it you will find values approximating a normal curve on the values continuum. Those in the center are values you would ordinarily intend in that circumstance. Those on the left end of the continuum are values you could enact even under stress and those on the right end of the continuum values you envision and to which you aspire.

The process of identifying your particular profile on a values continuum is a process of discernment—choosing/deciding in a reflective context. The following process is useful in determining your particular value profile in a given situation.

1. Select a positive experience in your personal history and relive that experience in all sensory channels, see, hear, feel, smell and taste.

2. Select a negative experience in your personal history and relive that experience in all sensory channels, see, hear, feel, smell and taste.

3. Check all the values operative in both experiences on the values list, figure 47.

4. Select the fifteen (15) most important to you from among those checked and write them in the space provided on figure 47.

5. Prioritize the fifteen (15) you selected, with one (1) the most important and fifteen (15) the least important.

6. Locate the values you selected on the value continuum and record them on the values profile in the space for individual profile in figure 50.

7. If several people as a group are constructing a values profile, figure 50, can be used to construct a group profile as well.

---

*Brian P. Hall and Benjamin Tonna, *God's Plan For Us* (New York: Paulist Press, 1980), page 32.

Values List

SELECTED VALUES

SPECIFIC VALUES

1. Accountability/Mutual Responsibility
2. Achievement/Success
3. Adaptability/Flexibility
4. Administration/Control
5. Affection/Physical
6. Art/Beauty/As Pure Value
7. (Self) Assertion
8. Being Liked
9. Being Self
10. Care/Nurture
11. (Self) Centeredness
12. Communications
13. Community/Personalist
14. Community/Supportive
15. Competition
16. (Self) Competence/Confidence
17. Congruence
18. Construction/New Order
19. Contemplation/Asceticism
20. (Self) Control
21. Control/Order/Discipline
22. Convivial Tools/Intermediate Technology
23. Cooperation
24. Corporation/Construction/New Order
25. Courtesy/Respect
26. Creativity/Ideation
27. Criteria/Rationality
28. (Self) Delight
29. Detachment/Solitude
30. Decision/Initiation
31. Design/Pattern/Order
32. (Self) Directedness
33. Discovery/Delight
34. Discernment/Communal
35. Duty/Obligation
36. Economics/Profit
37. Economics/Success
38. Ecority/Beauty/Aesthetics
39. Education/Certification
40. Education/Knowledge/Insight
41. Efficiency/Planning
42. Empathy
43. Equilibrium
44. Equality/Liberation
45. Equity/Rights
46. Ethics/Accountability/Values
47. Evaluation/Self-System
48. Expressiveness/Freedom
49. Faith/Risk
50. Family/Belonging
51. Fantasy/Play
52. Food/Warmth/Shelter
53. Friendship/Belonging
54. Function
55. Generosity/Service
56. Growth/Expansion
57. Harmony/System
58. Health/Personal
59. Hierarchy/Propriety/Order
60. Honor
61. Human Dignity
62. Independence
63. Instrumentality
64. Integration/Wholeness
65. Interdependence
66. Intimacy
67. Intimacy/Solitude as unitive
68. Justice
69. Knowledge/Discovery/Insight
70. Law/Guide
71. Law/Rule
72. Life/Self-Actualization
73. Limitation/Celebration
74. Loyalty/Respect
75. Macro Economics
76. Management
77. Membership/Institution
78. Mission/Goals
79. Obedience/Duty
80. Obedience/Mutual Accountability
81. Objectivity
82. Ownership
83. Patriotism/Esteem
84. Pioneerism/Innovation/Progress
85. Play/Leisure
86. Pluriformity
87. Poverty/Simplicity
88. Power Authority/Honesty
89. Presence/Dwelling
90. (Self) Preservation
91. Prestige/Image
92. Productivity
93. Property/Control
94. Recreation/Freesence
95. Relaxation
96. Research/Originality/Knowledge
97. Responsibility
98. Ritual/Meaning
99. Rule/Accountability
100. Safety/Survival
101. Search/Meaning
102. Security
103. Sensory Pleasure/Sex
104. Service/Vocation
105. Sharing/Listening/Trust
106. Simplicity/Play
107. Social Affirmation
108. Support (Peer)
109. Synergy
110. Tradition
111. Transcendence/Global Confluence
112. Truth/Wisdom/Intuitive Insight
113. Unity/Solidarity
114. Wonder/Awe/Fate
115. Wonder/Curiosity
116. Word
117. Work/Labor
118. Workmanship/Craft
119. Worship/Duty/Creed
120. (Self) Worth

Figure 47. Values list.

Hall, Brian P., and Tonna, Benjamin. GOD'S PLAN FOR US. (New York: Paulist Press, 1980), p. 117, used with permission.

The Four Phases in the Development of Consciousness

ELEMENTS IN CONSCIOUSNESS	PHASE I	PHASE II	PHASE III	PHASE IV
How THE WORLD is perceived by the individual.	The world is a MYSTERY over which I have NO CONTROL.	The world is a PROBLEM with which I must COPE.	The World is a PROJECT in which I must PARTICIPATE.	The World is a MYSTERY for which WE must CARE.
How the individual perceives its SELF FUNCTION in the world.	The self EXISTS at the center of a HOSTILE WORLD. The self struggles to SURVIVE in an ALIEN, OPPRESSIVE, CAPRICIOUS ENVIRONMENT.	The self DOES things to succeed and to belong in a SOCIAL WORLD. The self seeks TO BELONG in a SIGNIFICANT HUMAN ENVIRONMENT and TO BE APPROVED by other SIGNIFICANT PERSONS.	The self ACTS on the CREATED WORLD with conscience and independence. The self strives TO RESHAPE the NATURAL, SOCIAL, CULTURAL ENVIRONMENTS with CONSCIENCE and INDEPENDENCE	SELVES GIVE LIFE to the GLOBAL WORLD. Selves ENLIVEN the GLOBAL ENVIRONMENT through the UNION of INTIMACY and SOLITUDE within and the HARMONY of SYSTEMS without.
What HUMAN NEEDS the self seeks to satisfy.	The self seeks to satisfy the PHYSICAL NEED for FOOD, PLEASURE/SEX, WARMTH, and SHELTER.	The self seeks to satisfy the SOCIAL NEED for ACCEPTANCE, AFFIRMATION, APPROVAL, ACHIEVEMENT.	The self seeks to satisfy the PERSONAL NEED to EXPRESS CREATIVE INSIGHTS, BE ONESELF, DIRECT ONE'S LIFE, AND OWN ONE'S IDEAS/ENTERPRISES.	Selves seek to satisfy the COMMUNAL NEED for GLOBAL HARMONY by nurturing persons and communities from their phase of consciousness.

The Eight Stages in the Development of Values

KINDS OF CORE VALUES	STAGE I A	STAGE I B	STAGE II A	STAGE II B	STAGE III A	STAGE III B	STAGE IV A	STAGE IV B
Values which are ENDS in themselves.	Self-Preservation	Security	Family/ Belonging Self-Worth	Self Competence/ Confidence	Life/Self-Actualization Service/Vocation	Being Self Human Dignity	Intimacy/ Solitude	Ecority/Beauty Transcendence
Values which are MEANS to Ends Values.	Safety/ Survival		Instrumentality	Education	Empathy Health Independence	Accountability/ Mutual Responsibility	Inter-dependence	Convivial Tools/ Intermediate Technology

Figure 48. Developmental continuum.

Hall, Brian P., and Tonna, Benjamin. GOD'S PLANS FOR US. (New York: Paulist Press, 1980). p. 36, used with permission.

Value Continuum

	PHASE I		PHASE II		PHASE III		PHASE IV	
	A [Primary]	**B [Primary]**	**A [Primary]**	**B [Primary]**	**A [Primary]**	**B [Primary]**	**A [Primary]**	**B [Primary]**
	(Self) Centeredness *(Self) Preservation Wonder/Awe/Fate	(Self) Delight *Security	(Self) Control **Family/Belonging Fantasy/Play *(Self) Worth	Play/Leisure *Self Competence/Confidence Work/Labor Worship/Duty/Creed	Equality/Liberation Integration/Wholeness *Life/Self Actualization *Service/Vocation	Art/Beauty/As Pure Value *Being Self Construction/New Order Contemplation/Asceticism *Human Dignity Knowledge/Discovery Insight Presence/Dwelling Ritual/Meaning	Harmony/System Personal *Intimacy and solitude as unitive (Union) Truth/Wisdom/Intuitive Insight	*Ecority/Beauty Aesthetics *Transcendence/Global Congruence Harmony/System
	A [Means]	**B [Means]**	**A [Means]**	**B [Means]**	**A [Means]**	**B [Means]**	**A [Means]**	**B [Means]**
	Food/Warmth/Shelter **Safety/Survival	Affection/Physical Discover/Delight Economics/Profits Property/Control Sensory Pleasure/Sex Wonder/Curiosity	Being Liked Care/Nurture Competition Control/Order/Discipline Courtesy/Respect Equilibrium Friendship/Belonging Function **Instrumentality Obedience/Duty Prestige/Image Social Affirmation Support (Peer) Tradition	Achievement/Success Administration/Control Communications Competition Control/Order/Discipline Criteria/Rationality Design/Pattern/Order Duty/Obligation Economics/Success *Education (Certification) Efficiency/Planning Hierarchy/Property/Order Honor	Adaptability/Flexibility (Self) Assertion Congruence Decision/Initiation (Self) Directedness **Empathy Equity/Rights Evaluation/Self System Expressiveness/Freedom Generosity/Service **Health (Personal) **Independence Law/Guide Limitation/Celebration Obedience/Mutual	**Accountability/Mutual Responsibility Community/Supportive Corporation/Construction/New Order Creativity/Ideation Detachment/Solitude Discernment Education/Knowledge/Insight Ethics/Accountability/Values	Community/Personalist **Interdependence Synergy Word	**Convivial tools/Intermediate Technology Macro Economics

Value Continuum—*Continued*

PHASE I	PHASE II	PHASE III	PHASE IV
	Instrumentality	Accountability	
	Law/Rule	Power/Authority/	
	Loyality/Respect	Honesty	
	Management	Relaxation Search/	
	Membership/	Meaning	
	Institution	Sharing/Listening/	
	Objectivity	Trust	
	Ownership		
	Patriotism/Esteem		
	Productivity		
	Responsibility		
	Rule/		
	Accountability		
	Workmanship/		
	Craft		
	Unity/Solidarity		

Growth/Expansion
Intimacy
Justice
Mission/Goals
Pioneerism/
Innovation/
Progress
Pluriformity
Poverty/Simplicity
Recreation/
Freesence
Research/
Originality
Knowledge
Simplicity/Play
Cooperation
Faith/Risk

Figure 49. Value continuum.

*Core Values
**Prime Skill Values
Hall, Brian P., and Tonna, Benjamin. GOD'S PLANS FOR US. (New York: Paulist Press, 1980.) Appendix A, used with permission.

Group Values Profile

	PHASE I		PHASE II		PHASE III		PHASE IV	
	A	B	A	B	A	B	A	B
Primary								
Means								

Individual Values Profile

	PHASE I		PHASE II		PHASE III		PHASE IV	
	A	B	A	B	A	B	A	B
Primary								
Means								

Figure 50. Values profile — individual and group.

162

Bibliography

Alberti, Robert E., and Emmons, Michael L. *Stand Up, Speak Out, Talk Back!* New York: Pocket Books, 1975.

————. *Your Perfect Rights: A Guide to Assertive Behavior.* 2nd ed. San Luis Obispo, Calif.: Impact Press, 1974.

Auvine, Brian, et al. *A Manual for Group Facilitators.* Madison, Wis.: Center for Conflict Resolution, 1978.

Bandler, Richard, and Grinder, John. *Frogs into Princes.* Moab, Utah: Real People Press, 1979.

————. *The Structure of Magic I.* Palo Alto, Calif.: Science and Behavior Books, 1975.

Berne, Eric. *Games People Play.* New York: Dell Publishing, 1964.

Blake, Robert R., and Mouton, Jane S. *Corporate Excellence Through GRID Organization Development.* Houston, Texas: Gulf Publishing Company, 1971.

Carkhuff, Robert R. *The Development of Human Resources.* New York: Holt, Rinehart and Winston, 1971.

Carkhuff, Robert R.; Berenson, D. H.; and Pierce, R. M. *The Skills of Teaching Interpersonal Skills.* Amherst, Mass.: Human Resource Development Press, 1977.

Coser, Lewis. *The Functions of Social Conflict.* New York: Macmillan Company, 1956.

Deutsch, Morton. *The Resolution of Conflict: Constructive and Destructive Processes.* New Haven, Conn.: Yale University Press, 1973.

————. "A Theory of Cooperation and Competition." *Human Relations* 2 (1949): 129–52.

————. "Trust and Suspicion." *Journal of Conflict Resolution* 2 (1958): 265–79.

Egan, Gerard. *Interpersonal Living: A Skills/Contract Approach to Human Relations Training in Groups.* Monterey, Calif.: Brooks/Cole, 1976.

————. *The Skilled Helper: A Model for Systematic Helping and Interpersonal Relations.* Monterey, Calif.: Brooks/Cole, 1975.

Filley, Alan C. *Interpersonal Conflict Resolution.* Glenview, Ill.: Scott, Foresman and Company. 1975.

Fisher, B. Aubry. *Small Group Decision-Making: Communication and the Group Process.* New York: McGraw-Hill, 1974.

Fisher, Roger, and Ury, William. *Getting to Yes: Negotiating Agreement Without Giving In.* Boston, Mass.: Houghton Mifflin Company, 1981.

Galper, Jeffry. "Nonverbal Communication Exercises in Groups." *Social Work* 15 (April 1970): 71–78.

Gaylin, Willard. *Feelings.* New York: Harper and Row, Publishers, 1979.

Gazda, George M. *Human Relations Development: A Manual for Educators.* Boston, Mass.: Allyn and Bacon Publishing, 1973.

Goldstein, Arnold P. *Prevention and Control of Aggression.* New York: Pergamon Press, 1983.

Goldstein, Arnold P., and Rosenbaum, Alan. *Aggressless.* Englewood Cliffs, N.J.: Prentice-Hall, 1982.

Gordon, Thomas. *Leadership Effectiveness Training.* New York: Wyden Publishing, 1977.

————. *Parent Effectiveness Training.* New York: Wyden Publishing, 1970.

Hall, Brian P., and Thompson, Helen. *Leadership Through Values.* New York: Paulist Press, 1980.

Hall, Brian P., and Tonna, Benjamin. *God's Plans for Us.* New York: Paulist Press, 1980.

Hall, Jay. *Conflict Management Survey: A Survey of One's Characteristic Reaction to and Handling of Conflict Between Himself and Others.* The Woodlands, Texas: Telemetrics International, 1969.

Harmin, Merrill; Kirschenbaum, H.; and Simon, S. B. *Clarifying Values Through Subject Matter.* Minneapolis, Minn.: Winston Press, 1973.

Himes, Joseph S. *Conflict and Conflict Management.* Athens, Ga.: University of Georgia Press, 1980.

Jakubowski, Patricia, and Lange, Arthur. *The Assertive Option.* Chicago, Ill.: Research Press Co., 1978.

Kelley, Colleen. *Assertion Training: A Facilitators Guide*. San Diego, Calif.: University Associates, Inc., 1979.

Kriesberg, Louis. *Social Conflict*. 2nd ed. Englewood Cliffs, N.J.: Prentice-Hall, 1983.

Laborde, Genie Z. *Influencing With Integrity*. Palo Alto: Syntony Inc. Publishing Co., 1984.

Lange, Arthur, and Jakubowski, Patricia. *Responsible Assertive Behavior*. Champaign, Ill.: Research Press, 1976.

Lawyer, John W., and Livingston, Patricia H. *Communication Skills*. Pompey, N.Y.: Henneberry Hill Consultants, Inc., 1977.

Lewin, Kurt. *Resolving Social Conflict*. New York: Harper and Brothers Publishers, 1948.

Lippit, Gordon L. *Visualizing Change*. LaJolla, Calif.: Learning Resources Corporation/University Associates, 1973.

Lisbe, Ed. *Assertion Messages*. Unpublished manuscript made available by the author, 1980.

Luft, Joseph. *Of Human Interaction*. Palo Alto, Calif.: National Press Books, 1969.

Margulis, Joel, and Richardson, Jerry. *The Magic of Rapport: The Business of Negotiation*. New York: Avon Books, 1981.

Maslow, Abraham. *Self-Actualization*. San Fernando, Calif.: Superscope Library, 1972.

Mayeroff, Milton. *On Caring*. New York: Harper and Row, 1971.

McClelland, David C. *Power: The Inner Experience*. New York: Irvington Publishers, Inc., 1975.

Miller, Gerald R. *Explorations in Interpersonal Communication*. Beverly Hills, Calif.: Sage Publications, 1976.

Miller, Gerald R., and Simons, Herbert W. eds. *Perspectives on Communication in Social Conflict*. Englewood Cliffs, N.J.: Prentice-Hall, 1974.

Myers, J. Gordon. *Problem Solving*. Unpublished manuscript made available by the author, 1980.

Nierenberg, Gerard I. *The Art of Negotiating*. New York: Cornerstone Library, 1981.

————. *Fundamentals of Negotiating*. New York: Hawthorne Books, 1973.

Patton, Bobby R., and Gi-fin, Kim. *Decision Making Group Interaction*. 2nd ed. New York: Harper and Row, 1978.

Plutchik, Robert. "A Language for the Emotions." *Psychology Today* 13 (February 1980): 68–78.

Prince, George M. *The Practice of Creativity*. New York: Collier Books, 1970.

Rokeach, Milton. *The Open and Closed Mind*. New York: Basic Books, Inc., 1960.

Schein, Edgar, H. *Process Consultation*. Reading, Mass.: Addison-Wesley Publishing Company, 1961.

Simon, Sidney B., et al. *Values Clarification*. New York: Hart Publishing Company, 1972.

Smith, Clagett G. *Conflict Resolution: Contributions of the Behavioral Sciences*. Notre Dame, Ind.: University of Notre Dame Press, 1971.

Stanford, Barbara. *Peacemaking: A Guide to Conflict Resolution for Individuals, Groups and Nations* New York: Bantam, 1975.

Stein, Arthur A. "Conflict and Cohesion: A Review of the Literature." *Journal of Conflict Resolution* 20 (March 1976): 143–72.

Steven, John O. *Awareness*. New York: Bantam Books, 1973.

Swingle, Paul. *The Structure of Conflict*. New York: Academic Press, 1970.

Vandt, Fred E. *Conflict Resolution Through Communication*. New York: Harper and Row, 1973.

Walton, Richard E. *Inter-personal Peacemaking: Confrontation and Third-Party Consultation*. Reading, Mass.: Addison-Wesley, 1969.

Wehr, Paul. *Conflict Regulation*. Boulder, Colo.: Westview Press, 1979.

Wilmot, William W. and Hocker, Joyce L. *Interpersonal Conflict*. New York: William C. Brown Company Publishers, 2nd ed., 1985.

Wilson, Marlene. *Survival Skills for Managers*. Boulder, Colo.: Volunteer Management Associates, 1981.

NOTES

NOTES